101

BOOKS BY ANNE MICHAELS

POETRY

The Weight of Oranges (1986)

Miner's Pond (1991)

Skin Divers (1999)

FICTION

Fugitive Pieces (1996)

Poems

P o e m s

The Weight of Oranges

Miner's Pond

Skin Divers

by

Anne Michaels

ALFRED A. KNOPF   NEW YORK   2000

The Weight of Oranges, copyright © 1986 by Anne Michaels
Miner's Pond, copyright © 1991 by Anne Michaels
Skin Divers, copyright © 1999 by Anne Michaels

The Weight of Oranges was originally published by The Coach House Press, Toronto, Canada, in 1986.
Miner's Pond was originally published by McClelland & Stewart, Inc., Toronto, Canada, in 1991.
Skin Divers was originally published by McClelland & Stewart, Inc., Toronto, Canada, in 1999.

Following is a list of the magazines and anthologies where some of the poems in this volume first appeared: From *The Weight of Oranges: Writ, Waves, Poetry Toronto,* and *Poetry Canada Review.* From *Miner's Pond: Saturday Night, The Malahat Review,* and *What* magazine. From *Skin Divers: Border Crossing, Event, Toronto Life, Windhorse Reader, Slow Dancer, Fish Drum, We Who Can Fly, Border Lines: Contemporary Poems in English.*

Grateful acknowledgment is made to the following for permission to reprint previously published material:
RENDITIONS PAPERBACKS: Excerpt from the poem "A Second Farewell at the Feng-chi Post-station" by Tu Fu, in *A Little Primer of Tu Fu,* translated by David Hawkes (Hong Kong: Research Centre for Translation of The Chinese University of Hong Kong, Renditions Paperbacks, 1987, 1994). Copyright © 1987 by The Chinese University of Hong Kong. Reprinted by permission of the publisher. RANDOM HOUSE, INC.: Excerpt from "Canzone" by W. H. Auden, from *Collected Poems of W. H. Auden,* edited by Edward Mendelson (New York: Random House, Inc.), copyright © 1976, 1991 by The Estate of W. H. Auden. Reprinted by permission of the publisher.

ISBN: 0-375-40140-7

Manufactured in the United States
First United States Edition

The three books collected here were originally published separately, but were written as companion volumes. I'm grateful to Harry Ford for his invitation to publish them together, and for his long-standing enthusiasm for this project.

This edition of Poems *remembers Harry Ford, with many thanks.*

Contents

Miner's Pond (1991)

Skin Divers (1999)

I

II

III

The Weight
of Oranges

For Rosalind and Isaiah Michaels

I

Lake of Two Rivers

1

Pull water, unhook its seam.

Lie down in the lake room,
in the smell of leaves still sticky from their birth.

Fall to sleep the way the moon falls
from earth: perfect lethargy of orbit.

2

Six years old, half asleep,
a traveller. The night car mysterious
as we droned past uneasy twisting fields.

My father told two stories on these drives.
One was the plot of *Lost Horizon*,
the other: his life.
This speeding room, dim in the dashboard's green emission,
became the hijacked plane carrying Ronald Colman to Tibet,
or the train carrying my father across Poland in 1931.

Spirit faces crowded the windows of a '64 Buick.
Unknown cousins surrounded us, arms around each other,
a shawl of sleeves.

The moon fell into our car from Grodno.
It fell from Chaya-Elke's village,
where they stopped to say goodbye.

His cousin Mashka sat up with them
in the barn, while her face
floated down the River Neman in my father's guitar.
He watched to remember
in the embalming moonlight.

3

Sensate weather, we are your body,
your memory. Like a template,
branch defines sky, leaves
bleed their gritty boundaries,
corrosive with nostalgia.

Each year we go outside to pin it down,
light limited, light specific,
light like a name.

•

For years my parents fled at night,
loaded their children in the back seat,
a tangle of pyjamas anxious to learn the stars.

I watched the backs of their heads
until I was asleep, and when I woke
it was day, and we were in Algonquin.

I've always known this place,
familiar as a room in our house.

The photo of my mother, legs locked in water,
looking into the hills where you and I stand—
only now do I realize
it was taken before I was born.

•

Purple mist, indefinite hills.

At Two Rivers, close as branches.
Fish scatter, silver pulses with their own electric logic.

Milky spill of moon over the restless lake,
seen through a sieve of foliage.

In fields to the south
vegetables radiate underground,
displace the earth.
While we sit, linked by firelight.

4

The longer you look at a thing
the more it transforms.

My mother's story is tangled,
overgrown with lives of parents and grandparents
because they lived in one house and among them
remembered hundreds of years of history.

This domestic love is plain, hurts
the way light balancing objects in a still life hurts.

The heart keeps body and spirit in suspension,
until density pulls them apart.
When she was my age
her mother had already fallen through.

Pregnant, androgynous with man,
she was afraid. When life goes out,
loss gets in, wedging a new place.

Under dark lanes of the night sky
the eyes of our skin won't close,
we dream in desire.

Love wails from womb, caldera, home.
Like any sound, it goes on forever.

                    •

The dissolving sun turns Two Rivers into skin.
Our pink arms, slightly fluorescent,
hiss in the dusky room, neon tubes bending
in the accumulated dark.

Night transforms the lake into a murmuring solid.
Naked in the eerie tremor of leaves rubbing stars,
in the shivering fermata of summer,
in the energy of stones made powerful by gravity,
desire made powerful by the seam between starlight and skin,
we join, moebius ribbon in the night room.

5

We do not descend, but rise from our histories.
If cut open, memory would resemble
a cross-section of the earth's core,
a table of geographical time.
Faces press the transparent membrane
between conscious and genetic knowledge.
A name, a word, triggers the dilatation.
Motive is uncovered, sharp overburden in a shifting field.

·

When I was twenty-five I drowned in the River Neman,
fell through when I read that bone-black from the ovens
was discarded there.

Like a face pressed against a window,
part of you waits up for them,
like a parent, you wait up.

·

A family now, we live each other's life
without the details.

The forest flies apart, trees are shaken loose
by my tears,

by love that doesn't fall to earth
but bursts up from the ground, fully formed.

II

The Day of Jack Chambers

The day of Jack Chambers
we are black smudges on the frozen river.
You're walking ahead—in summer I would've said "upstream"—
sky, blue of veins, air the palest skin.
Old February light, weakest of the year,
casting its tinge like light in paintings
when the varnish has aged.
You're halfway up the river,
it's five o'clock and I can tell
by the way your back's to me, you're measuring pigments,
stealing the contents of this light, and sure enough
it begins to get dark.

We spent the day looking at Chambers' paintings.
Even the earliest have the magnification of dying.
Ten years of leukemia, you have to think what you fear,
not just be afraid.
When he worked from photos
he added what happened before the shutter was pressed—
and what happened after.
Objects hang in the air where they'd been the moment before,
floating like dust in sunlight.
Always the same light—captive, gasping to get out
from Sunday place settings, his wife's hair,
from chrome trim and roofs of cars on the highway.

You explained visual time,
how there's no weight without shadow.
Nothing falls, every figure has a ghostly buoyancy.
You explained how Chambers grounded things with his light,

leaving the ghost inside.
I understood this by thinking "language" instead of "light,"
how everything suspended stays temporal.
I understood it as a grammar of beauty
with its apex of loss,
dishevelled burning trees half leafless.
As a room full of rain and the raft of our bed.
The way we fall from each other like halves of an orange,
skin dark as pottery in lamplight.
I know it, naked in the light of the fridge,
cold plummy resins in our mouths, warm sticky resins
of our bodies. By nights
we drain the pictures from your head and words
from my throat until I find nothing but sounds there.
And today, by way of light closing around itself
until the river is dark and all I see is your white breath.
By way of a young woman's hunger
to taste every part of her lover, even his words.

Chambers' painting of a girl: if the light were stronger
you'd see her bones, the green-blue tributaries
beginning and returning at the heart.
And the sky that's "wrong,"
cloud-mottled, above the horizon,
yet painted as if we're looking straight up.
Your brain tricks you,
like losing your balance in a dream,
being woken by the feeling of falling.

What you paint
are the parts left behind
when two people join.
Your figures look calm,
but their throats are closed
with cries that can't get out.
They are in mourning.
Your canvas finds a weakness in the air's tension,
someone's past seeps out.
We arrive by accumulation.
Time twists us by the shoulders until we're positioned to die,
looking backwards. Twisted into the ground.

Night. Soon we are pushing our faces
into the bin of stars. Lamplight
melts the windows of the river houses.
I can feel your bony fingers in your gloves.

This day belongs to Chambers. This
his river, his light. His eyes
that watched your black figure on the river,
sky the blue of veins, air
a translucent skin over everything.

There are three kinds of teachers, you said.
One who teaches by making you afraid,
one who makes you angry.
The third makes you love him.

Anna

Nothing moved except a green fern pushing its way out of a jar.
In our house, truths were told in the kitchen,
always in the hum of the fridge and in half darkness:
early evening, with what was left of light gathered on rims of things,
or in the pale vibrato light before sunrise
after we'd left our warm bed
and made our way to the kitchen table.

That summer we sat on the porch as if waiting,
as if we knew it was ending.
We waved to Anna, sixteen, in white shorts and sneakers,
already halfway down the street and not looking back.
She flew like a moth into those soft evenings,
restless in the strange mixture
of twilight and the light of streetlamps.

One night we drove to the lakeshore,
past the powerful debris at the harbour,
rows of bins and trucks, train tracks, factories.
Past places we never see inside of.
We watched the water until midnight
and never knew Anna was with us,
calling out in the fish-burnt air,
calling from the shiny embrace that closed around her as it opened.
No one heard.
Boat lights on the surface like the rim of light beneath a door.

She floated, rigid as driftwood to the brim of the lake.
Two miles from where we sat, in the night's slow annulment of colour,
gulls like winter breaths close to the water.

Endings concur: a crossroad.
Grief strikes where love struck first.
Our last morning together we sat with Anna's family in dark rooms.
We watched her mother put a sweater in the coffin.
These are endings that bind,
love still alive, squirming in the rind of the heart.

A voice we don't recognize calls up from ourselves.
We move in closer, trying to make out the words.
That begins love, or ends it—we start to make out the words.
We give to save ourselves. We forgive to save ourselves.

We recognize death and love when we can start calling them names.
Each other's.
The name of a young girl turned ugly by our deafness.

A Height of Years

in memory of Frank Gordon

1

The small ship of his bones sinks in the earth.
I cry for my father because of everyone's short sleeves,
the paleness of arms in the first strong sunlight.
Beyond the gate, shirts on a line
point their empty sleeves at us.
Warm spring wind, mud drying under our shoes.

My brother and I stand in the lane
behind the house where we grew up.
We stare, our hands on the wooden fence,
trying to see in through a kitchen window.
We fall from a height of years,
swooping like birds within an inch of the lawn.

2

Old glass wavers the lane, the red garages.
November, season of half days,
slips under the door like an envelope.
Cold floors.
A tangled black tree cuts shapes into a white sky,
makes the yard mysterious as it withdraws
under a black pattern of birds
joined in motive and rhythm,
a black arrow pointing south.
The house withdraws under their high cries,

a red roof among half-bare branches, a twist of smoke.
Soon, just smoke.

Daylight fades the colour of cut fruit rusting.
Leaves give way at their dry wrists.

3

The tarred street becomes a black eel
in the downpour. We watch from the porch,
peeled paint and caked mud scratching our legs.
Rain unearths the dusty smell of lilacs.
Old dandelions collapse into fine ash over the lawn.
The rain stops, drips inconsistently
from an edge of awning.
After supper the street turns molten
under the yellow pollen of moonlight.

4

Every house is a storehouse.
We came back to stand under ours while it fell,
to sit in the debris, to be in the burning place.
We looked out of windows and sat on the porch
while it rained.

5

We become inaccurate.
Someone you love with tubes down his throat
shows you every way you can't love him.
Blood, that euphemism for what moves in us.

Memoriam

In lawnchairs under stars. On the dock
at midnight, anchored by winter clothes,
we lean back to read the sky. Your face white
in the womb light, the lake's electric skin.

Driving home from Lewiston, full and blue, the moon
over one shoulder of highway. There,
or in your kitchen at midnight, sitting anywhere
in the seeping dark, we bury them again and
again under the same luminous thumbprint.

The dead leave us starving with mouths full of love.

Their stones are salt and mark where we look back.
Your mother's hand at the end of an empty sleeve,
scratching at your palm, drawing blood.
Your aunt in a Jewish graveyard in Poland,
her face a permanent fist of pain.
Your first friend, Saul, who died faster than
you could say forgive me.
When I was nine and crying from a dream
you said words that hid my fear.
Above us the family slept on,
mouths open, hands scrolled.
Twenty years later your tears burn the back of my throat.
Memory has a hand in the grave up to the wrist.
Earth crumbles from your fist under the sky's black sieve.
We are orphaned, one by one.

On the beach at Superior, you found me
where I'd been for hours, cut by the lake's sharp rim.

You stopped a dozen feet from me.
What passed in that quiet said:
I have nothing to give you.

At dusk, birch forest is a shore of bones.
I've pulled stones from the earth's black pockets,
felt the weight of their weariness—worn,
exhausted from their sleep in the earth.
I've written on my skin with their black sweat.

The lake's slight movement is stilled by fading light.
Soon the stars' tiny mouths, the moon's blue mouth.

I have nothing to give you, nothing to carry,
some words to make me less afraid, to say
you gave me this.
Memory insists with its sea voice,
muttering from its bone cave.
Memory wraps us
like the shell wraps the sea.
Nothing to carry,
some stones to fill our pockets,
to give weight to what we have.

Turning Twenty-three

You turned twenty-two in the rain.
We walked in rubber boots
along Lowther, the street shiny as albumen
under streetlamps.

At midnight, the sky suddenly clear,
we drove your jazz-filled car
through cold pungent streets to the lake
where we collected stones by flashlight.
The wind wrapped us in its torsions,
we couldn't hear each other although we shouted,
wet with star-swallowing waves.

By morning the stones we'd found
were dull with air,
but I couldn't forget the smell
of the trees' small darkness,
the scattered sound of the rain's distracted hands,
husks of buds in green pools on the sidewalks.

To love one person above all others
is despair, you said, turning twenty-two.
Propaganda of the senses, the narrow-minded heart—

Above the corrugated, elastic lake
a darkening sky holds out its arms.
I repeat your name, each time different,
into sand, into moonlight.
A thousand miles away, you're turning twenty-three.
The sky holds out its arms.

Depth of Field

*"The camera relieves us of the burden of memory . . .
records in order to forget."*
—JOHN BERGER

We've retold the stories of our lives
by the time we reach Buffalo,
sun coming up diffuse and prehistoric
over the Falls.

A white morning,
sun like paint on the windshield.
You drive, smoke, wear sunglasses.

Rochester, Camera Capital of America.
Stubbing a cigar in the lid of a film canister,
the Kodak watchman gives directions.

The museum's a wide-angle mansion.
You search the second storey from the lawn,
mentally converting bathrooms to darkrooms.

A thousand photos later,
exhausted by second-guessing
the mind which invisibly surrounds each image,
we nap in a high school parking lot,
sun leaning low as the trees
over the roof of the warm car.

Driving home. The moon's so big and close
I draw a moustache on it and smudge the windshield.

I stick my fingers in your collar to keep you awake.
I can't remember a thing about our lives before this morning.

We left our city at night and return at night.
We buy pineapple and float quietly through the neighbourhood,
thick trees washing themselves in lush darkness,
or in the intimate light of streetlamps.
In summer the planet's heavy with smells of us,
stung with the green odour of gardens.
Heat won't leave the pavement
until night is almost over.

I've loved you all day.
We take the old familiar Intertwine Freeway,
begin the long journey towards each other
as to our home town with all its lights on.

Another Year

Another year and we're together,
crossing your glinting fields.

Five p.m. under a sky claimed in childhood,
claimed in streets connecting your house with mine,
home from another city,
another year of separation.

We pause in our metallic light
and talk—50, 15, 25 years old,
depending on the subject.
Traversed by the treeline,
your body in your mother's jacket.
Nothing breaks the restraint of this grid,
your face held in place by pines,
New Year's Eve, our conversation.

Each year the forest presses our dialogue
into another ring.
One day the wooden record will play itself;
we'll hear each time we chose
one past over another to extrapolate,
each time that path grew over.

Your brother skates on the pond,
moving like pen on paper.

Time emanates from our selves.
We run after it
like your retriever let go in a field:
part fluid muscle, part slung leash.

January

Greetings Giulio Clovio, to your health!

Today I finished the last panel—"January"—for Jonghelinck
and with the wheel's perfect movement
winter's in the sky again like a shadowy dye,
my footsteps in the wet snow followed me home.

How unlike your Rome. Here the light is dense
with smoke and complaints from the valley.
Mayken says even the hills want change these days.
I say nothing.
When people talk of gatherings and plans
I turn from them. Think what you will,
it's a different life having meat with your soup.

I found my vantage for "January" near Van Mander's,
above the pond. I tell you
sometimes my head aches from keeping the two worlds separate,
the landscape deeply still—even the crows
like stones on the branch—and our little flasks of life,
convulsed with blood and breathing.
Sometimes I feel their heartbeats when I paint,
regular, like a word repeated,
against the drone of the fields.
To clear my head, I focus on the foreground.
My link between life and death is that first figure,
who breathes, but is too large to move across the canvas.

For months after my visit with you
I painted only mountains.

When Martin came to see me
he laughed until he looked drunk
and shouted, "Well I know you swallowed the Alps,
but must you spit them out again?"
Now everyone in Antwerp repeats the joke.

There are no people in my mountains.
Why give them any smallness?
But you, with your Italian heart, would say
how sweeter the contrast,
how sweet man's varieties of pain and love
against that lazy infinity—
how long it's been since we argued!

It rubs my heart to think you'll never see the light
in my country, as you've shown me yours.
Perhaps we know only one place with certainty.
I know what you would say to this:
"Pieter, that place is your heart,"
and I say to you (with respect, of course)
how can this be?

My heart is everywhere. In the front room with Mayken,
and in Italy with you.
So I answer you in this hypothetical dialogue,
that this heart of yours must be God.
After a while you'll poke the fire
and drink from your favourite theme:
"impossible to paint well what you don't love"

and I'll answer with my own obsession,
that there's a feature of each face I love,
in each face, my own ugliness and imperfection
and those qualities I love for their striving,
their movement in the history of families.
So you'll laugh and ask:
"But do not those who are ugly
grow even uglier with time?"
Giulio, you're too quick for me.

Mayken asks why I won't paint her.
I don't know why,
except she's not everyone to me yet,
I can't make her human.

I painted all day and at night
I walked back to the place and looked down on the houses,
lamplight connecting the trees like fabric.
Standing in the damp breath of the forest
I looked in your direction.

Are you on your balcony now?
Tomorrow morning Carel will come for this letter.
Each day he travels I'll look south.

Send me some of your Italian light,
even if it's not mine, I still miss it.
Send me the kind we labelled "before dinner, June"
or "dawn, the day Pieter Brueghel left for home."

Women on a Beach

Light chooses white sails, the bellies of gulls.

Far away in a boat, someone wears a red shirt,
a tiny stab in the pale sky.

Your three bodies form a curving shoreline,
pink and brown sweaters, bare legs.

The beach glows grainy under the sun's copper pressure,
air the colour of tangerines.
One of you is sleeping, the wind's finger
on your cheek like a tendril of hair.

Night exhales its long held breath.
Stars puncture through.

At dusk you are a small soft heap, a kind of moss.
In the moonlight, a boulder of women.

Pushed into the Dark

You taught me the day comes
when, gorged with your own life,
you can't go further.

At the window,
far from what you want,
knowing you've built on a fault,
a false premise.
In prisons the door ahead won't open
until the one behind locks.
This is how we move men.
Even then, we don't want to go through.

I looked from your room at Mass General
to the city you loved, out to J's Deli
in the old market, to the Italian pool hall
where they serve cannoli at wrought iron tables.

The only experience unchanged by recollection
is horror.

Before your illness
I admired qualities, thinking this was love,
thinking deference was humility.

Time presses down and we panic,
become inventive.
The sky presses down on a field
until it bursts
into the distorted shapes of vegetables.

No husband, no family,
your pace was frenetic,
the city yours.

We learned to love each other's weaknesses,
though this wasn't love, but tenderness.

When I came to the hospital
I found another friend waiting by your bed,
eating chocolate bars for supper, crying.
When body or spirit is inconsolable,
one tries to comfort the other.
As if they were separate, insoluble.

There is mystery in how we love,
but not in why.
Like forgiveness, love is practical.

From your window
we looked out at the flickering city.
You wanted to put your finger on every point of light,
push it into darkness.

As if my body and not yours
were the abandoned one.
Drunk with violation,
I do not defer.

Near Ashdod

in memory of Yoav Shapiro

This morning your letter, blue square torn open
like the sea he entered.
"He was flying upside down and didn't know it.
At night the sea to him seemed to be the sky."
You wrote as if I knew him, twenty-five, in uniform.

Dead, he was movement.
Shrieking through water,
suddenly out of the element that kept him alive.
Gravity broken by an engine, safe in speed and altitude,
then tricked by a colour in the dark.

We don't trust suddenness,
not news, not split-second choices.
We move in our direction.
Events fall into place, or out of place,
one day we know which.
Twisting around in the darkness, we know which.
This morning a square of light on the kitchen floor,
the room behind me reflected in the kettle.
Yoav, you had no time.
You tore the commissure
and flew into the place you thought you were escaping.

Rain Makes Its Own Night

Rain makes its own night, long mornings with the lamps left on.
Lean beach grass sticks to the floor near your shoes,
last summer's pollen rises from damp metal screens.

This is order, this clutter that fills clearings between us,
clothes clinging to chairs, your shoes in a muddy grip.

The hard rain smells like it comes from the earth.
The human light in our windows, the orange stillness
of rooms seen from outside. The place we fall to alone,
falling to sleep. Surrounded by a forest's green assurance,
the iron gauze of sky and sea,
while night, the rain, pulls itself down through the trees.

Letters from Martha

I rip the envelope and I'm in Bangkok.
I rip the envelope and I'm in Varanasi
Allahabad Agra Delhi.
Christmas Greetings from the Katmandu Hotel.
I rip the envelope:
my kitchen reeks with saffron,
I'm in a smelly passage crowded with sari'd throngs,
rickshaws, market stalls.
You're at my table, eyes alive with wild boars,
"skinny tea wallahs" carrying clay cups,
streets parting in the wake of a cow,
its cud a cardboard box soggy from vegetables.
I'm sorting your letters,
trying to keep the chronology,
the terrain of your marriage—in one letter
"better than ever, I'm in love all over again"
in another, "torn between distance and desire."
In Rajasthan you're reading a letter from your mother,
a childhood friend getting married, a sister leaving home.
And you, in love with a place.
You hate to leave Nagaur
where they came from all corners of India,
exodus of camels to a cattle fair.
You describe slums decaying
in twilight the colours of silks.
Hating to leave Nagaur, torn between distance and desire.
I rip the blue envelope and hear the jangle of bracelets,

I'm trying to find whose wrist they belong to in the gaudy market,
the flashy sunlight,
and there, your Western face and red hair
above that Indian river.
You pour from these squares, these blue envoys.
And just when I feel I've lost you in the world,
I can't keep up,
your postcard comes with the words
"wait for me."

The Weight of Oranges

"Now I lodge in the cabbage patches
of the important . . .
Not much sleep under strange roofs
with my life far away . . ."
—OSIP MANDELSTAM

My cup's the same sand colour as bread.
Rain's the colour of a building across the street,
it's torn red dahlias
and ruined a book propped on the sill.

Rain articulates the skins of everything,
pink of bricks from the fire they baked in,
lizard green leaves,
the wrinkled tongues of pine cones.
It's accurate the way we never are,
bringing out what's best
without changing a thing.
Rain that makes beds damp,
our room a cave in the morning,
a tent in late afternoon,
ignites the sound of leaves we miss all winter.
The sound that pulled us to bed . . .
caught in the undertow of wind in wet leaves.

I'm writing in the sound we woke to,
curtains breathing into a half-dark room.

I'm up early now, walking.
Remember our walks, horizons like lips

barely red at dawn,
how kind the distance seemed?

Letters should be written to send news, to say
send me news, to say
meet me at the train station.
Not these dry tears, to honour us like a tomb.
I'm ashamed of our separation.
I wake in the middle of night and see "shame"
written in the air like in a Bible story.
I dreamed my skin was tattooed,
covered with the words that put me here,
covered in sores, in quarantine—and you know what?
I was afraid to light the lamp and look.

Your husband's a good builder—I burned
every house we had, with a few words to start the flames.
Words of wood,
they had no power of their own.
"The important" gave them meaning
and humble with gratitude
they exploded in my face.

Now we're like planets, holding to each other
from a great distance. When we lay down
oceans flexed their green muscles,
life got busy in the other hemisphere,
the globe tilted, bowing to our power!

Now we're hundreds of miles apart,
our short arms keep us lonely,
no one hears what's in my head.
I look old. I'm losing my hair.
Where does lost hair go in this world,
lost eyesight, lost teeth?
We grow old like rivers, get shrunk and doubled over
until we can't find the mouth of anything.

It's March, even the birds
don't know what to do with themselves.

Sometimes I'm certain those who are happy
know one thing more than us . . . or one thing less.
The only book I'd write again
is our bodies closing together.
That's the language that stuns,
scars, breathes into you.
Naked, we had voices!

I want you to promise
we'll see each other again,
you'll send a letter.
Promise we'll be lost together
in our forest, pale birches of our legs.

I hear your voice now—I know,
everyone knows promises come from fear.
People don't live past each other,
you're always here with me. Sometimes
I pretend you're in the other room
until it rains . . . and then
this is the letter I always write:
The letter I write
when they're keeping me from home.
I smell your supper steaming in the kitchen.
There are paper bags on the table
with their bottoms melted out
by rain and the weight of oranges.

III

Words for the Body

Landowska, overheard during a heated argument on interpretation:
"You play Bach your way, and I'll play him his way."

1

We knew we'd reached Dunn Lake
because the trees stopped.

Chilled and sweating under winter clothes
we stood in the damp degenerated afternoon.
We grew up waiting together by water,
frozen or free,
in summer under the cool shaggy umbra of firs,
or in the aquarium light of birches.

It's always been this way between us.
We reach lakes and then just stand there.
Silence fills us with silence.

2

When we were fourteen
you read to me about Landowska, who
"tottered the world and stopped the sun when she held a note."
We argued over interpretation
until we were sixteen and discovered Casals:
"the best musician learns to play what's not on the page."
We decided music is memory,
the way a word is the memory of its meaning.

.

The first time I knew what we were trying for
I was waiting on the back porch while you practised.
Piano flickered the leaves,
evening in perfect summer,
temperature the same inside and outside my body,
night a pigment in my skin.

In that swathing twilight
I knew you'd had a lover.
Everything became part of that new perception.
The yard disappeared.
Sudden as my sense of your body,
I knew you were attempting silence.
To move an audience
until they aren't listening.

We believed in our head's perfect version,
but you couldn't make your hands, and
I couldn't make my words, pronounce it.

Even now when I hear you play
I think of a lover, gasping at the gate
of another, who suddenly knows
love has no power to make it right.

3

The summer you stopped playing
we were driving home from the farm,
windows full of stars on the dark highway,
legs bare on vinyl seats, night air
cold and new as from the sea.

In a voice that came from the highway
you described the blackness where music waits,
tormenting until you draw it out,
a redemption.
Then the fear of forgetting notes
disappears, the fingers have a memory of their own.

You spoke of a kind of hunger
that makes pleasure perfect.
Then you said how it was to be opened
and tasted by a hall full of people.

When we reached home
you were crying.

Within a month you stopped playing.
You stopped sleeping.
Eighteen years old, exhausted,
holding to the idea of perfect sound.

End of summer, rainy morning,
your head in my hands.
Across the room a jar of flowers
made its small fire.
Curtains held their breath against the wet screens.

4

Dunn Lake.
We skied there gracelessly through the woods.
Desperate light pressured black trees
to hold their pose.
The moon reached under the ice
where the lake moved, obedient.

Night pressed its thumbs over our eyes.
Too dark to take the way we came, we went by road.

You reached the farmhouse ahead of me,
I saw your figure in the porch lights.

We ate watching the fire,
logs collapsing under the weight of flame,
flames collapsing with their own weight.

Almost no word spoken since our silence at the lake,
you said you'd play again.

Over two years since your hands were yours.

You asked, smiling,
face torn with shadows from the fire:
"haven't you given up the perfect word yet?"

          •

Fingers have a memory,
to read the familiar braille of another's skin.
The body has a memory:
the children we make,

places we've hurt ourselves,
sieves of our skeletons in the fat soil.
No words mean as much as a life.
Only the body pronounces perfectly
the name of another.

5

This morning your letter.
A photo of redwoods in winter,
the half-frozen pond.
Remember the way we walked each other home—
one block further, one block further—
the way we skated in the ravine,
late winter afternoon,
so cold the air seemed to magnify the world,
sky the colour of plums.

We sang in harmony on the ice, breath echoing white
under the bridge, our fifteen-year-old bodies
perfect and young under winter clothes,
warm from skating and singing,
trees along the ridge a black lace picket fence
against a plume of orange like a comet's tail
where the sun had been.

Remember climbing the hill, already dark, and stopping to hear
trees shake their branches,
how we'd enter your parents' warm house
in a daze of images.

Remember once, mauve and yellow tulips on the dining room table,
remember the music when we said
play those colours
and turned Bach's "Anna Magdalena" the colour of yellow,
the colour of mauve.

Remember that October, standing in your farm's back field,
half a mile apart, while daylight collapsed
under the weight of darkness, and trees
thick with burning leaves
shouldered the stars.
Music emerged from those moments, from air,
like a room's white dimension in the window at nightfall.

   •

Any discovery of form is a moment of memory,
existing as the historical moment—alone,
and existing in history—linear,
in music, in the sentence.
Each poem, each piece remembers us perfectly,
the way the earth remembers our bodies,
the way man and woman in their joining
remember each other before they were separate.

It's over twenty-five years and every love poem
says how your music and my words are the same:
praising the common air, the motive, the memory.

To praise memory is to praise the body.

And I find myself describing
the joining of hips and eyes,
the harbours of thighs and lips,

as the singing of two small bodies in a dark ravine,
as two small bodies
holding up the night sky in a winter field.

Miner's Pond

For Martin, Arlen, and Howard Michaels

Miner's Pond

in memory of Elie David Michaels

1

A caver under stalactites,
the moon searches the stars.

In the low field, pools turn to stone.
Starlight scratches the pond,
penetrates in white threads;
in a quick breath, it fogs into ice.
A lava of fish murmurs the tightening film.

The crow is darkness's calculation;
all absence in that black moment's ragged span.

·

Above Miner's Pond, geese break out of the sky's
pale shell. They speak non-stop, amazed
they've returned from the stars,
hundreds of miles to describe.

It's not that they're wild, but
their will is the same as desire.
The sky peels back under their blade.

Like a train trestle, something in us rattles.
All November, under their passing.

·

Necks stiff as compass needles,
skeletons filled with air;

osmosis of emptiness, the space in them
equals space.

Their flight is a stria, a certainty;
sexual, one prolonged
reflex.

Cold lacquering speed, feathers oiled by wind,
surface of complete transfluency.
The sky rides with tremors in the night's milky grain.

     ·

Windows freeze over like shallow ponds,
hexagonally blooming.
The last syrup of light boils out from under the lid
of clouds; sky the colour of tarnish.
Like paperweights, cows hold down the horizon.

Even in a place you know intimately,
each night's darkness is different.

They aren't calling down to us.
We're nothing to them, unfortunates
in our heaviness.
We watch at the edge of words.

At Miner's Pond we use the past
to pull ourselves forward; rowing.

2

It was the tambourine that pushed my father
over the edge in 1962. His patience
a unit of time we never learned to measure.
The threat to "drive into a post"
was a landmark we recognized and raced towards
with delirious intent,
challenging the sound barrier of the car roof.

We were wild with stories we were living.
The front seat was another time zone
in which my parents were imprisoned, and from which
we offered to rescue them, again and again.

That day we went too far.
They left us at the side of the road
above St. Mary's quarry. My mother insists
it was my father's idea, she never wanted to drive away,
but in retrospect, I don't believe her.

This was no penalty; drilled in wilderness protocol,
happy as scouts, my brothers
planned food and shelter.
The youngest, I knew they'd come back for us,
but wasn't sure.

Hot August, trees above the quarry like green flames,
dry grass sharpened by the heat, and
dusty yellow soil "dry as mummy skin,"

a description meant to torment me.

They were rockhounds howling in the plastic light
melting over fossil hills;
at home among eras.

It was fifteen minutes, maybe less,
and as punishment, useless.
But the afternoon of the quarry lives on,
a geological glimpse;
my first grasp of time,
not continuous present.

.

Their language took apart landscapes,
stories of sastrugi and sandstreams,
shelves and rain shadow.
Atoms vibrating to solids,
waves into colours. Everything stone
began to swirl. Did the land sink
or the sea rise? When my brothers told me
I'd never seen the stars, that light's too slow,
that looking up is looking back,
there was no holding on. Beyond my tilting room
night swarmed with forest eyes and flying rats,
insects that look like branches, reptiles like rocks.
Words like solfatara, solfatara,
slipping me down like terraced water, into sleep.

.

Full of worlds they couldn't keep to themselves,
my brothers were deviant programmers of nightmares.
Descriptions of families *just like ours*,
with tongues petrified and forks welded to their teeth,
who'd sat down to Sunday dinner
and were flooded by molten rock;
explorers gnawing on boots in the world's dark attic;
Stadacona's sons, lured onto Cartier's ship and held hostage,
never to see home again.

When the lights were out
my free will disappeared.
Eyes dry with terror, I plummeted
to the limbo of tormented sisters, that global sorority
with chapters in every quiet neighbourhood, linked by fear
of volcanic explosions and frostbite, polar darkness,
and kidnapping by Frenchmen.

·

The ritual walk to the bakery, Fridays
before supper. Guided by my eldest brother
through streets made unfamiliar by twilight,
a decade between us.
I learned about invisibility:
the sudden disappearance of Röntgen's skin—
his hand gone to bones—and the discovery of X-rays.
Pasteur's germs, milk souring on the doorsteps of Arbois,
and microbe-laden wine—"what kind of wine?"—

the word "microbe"
rolling in my brother's fourteen-year-old mouth
like an outstanding beaujolais.
On these walks, frogs came back to life with electricity.
Sheep were cured of sheep-sickness.
Father Time, Einstein, never wore a watch.
Galileo saw the smooth face of the moon
instantly grow old,
more beautiful for being the truth.
The Curies found what they'd been looking for
only after giving up; they opened the lab and saw the glow,
incorruptible residue, radiant stain!

In winter, Glenholme Avenue was already dark,
with glass trees, elms shivering in their ice-sleeves.
As we walked, the essence of fresh bread
whirled into the secular air,
the street hungry for its pure smell.

Even now, I wrap what's most fragile
in the long gauze of science.
The more elusive the truth,
the more carefully it must be carried.

Remembering those walks,
I think of Darwin—
"no object in nature could avoid his loving recognition"—
on the bunk of the *Beagle*,
green with sea-sickness and the vertigo
of time. He was away five years

but the earth aged by millions.
Greeting him at Falmouth dock, his father cried:
"Why the shape of his head has changed!"
Stepping from cold night into the bright house,
I knew I'd been given privileged information,
because the excitement in my brother's voice
was exclusive to the street, temporary,
a spell.

.

Brother love, like the old family boat
we call the tin can: dented, awkward,
but still able to slice the lake's pink skin.

.

A family is a study in plate-tectonics, flow-folding.
Something inside shifts; suddenly we're closer or apart.

There are things brothers and sisters know—
the kind of details a spy uses
to prove his identity—
fears that slide through childhood's long grass,
things that dart out later; and pleasures like toucans,
their brightness weighing down the boughs.

Who but a brother calls from another hemisphere
to read a passage describing the strange
blip in evolution, when reptiles looked like
"alligator-covered coffee tables,"
evolution's teenagers, with a "severe case of the jimjams

during the therapsid heyday"—
remembering those were the creatures we loved best,
with bulky limbs and backs like sails.

Memory is cumulative selection.
It's an undersea cable connecting one continent
to another,
electric in the black brine of distance.

   3

Migrating underground, miles below the path of the geese,
currents and pale gases
stray like ghosts through walls of rock.
Above and below, the way is known;
but here, we're blind.

The earth means something different now.
It never heals, upturned constantly.

Now stones have different names.

Now there's a darkness like the lakes of the moon;
you don't have to be close to see it.

   •

My brother's son lived
one fall, one spring.

We're pushed outside, towards open fields,
by the feeling he's trying to find us.

Overhead the geese are a line,
a moving scar. Wavering
like a strand of pollen on the surface of a pond.
Like them, we carry each year in our bodies.
Our blood is time.

II

Sublimation

Since the day he followed me into the train station,
uniform under his coat,
I've had no language.

Stuttgart to Paris in your car,
no belongings or papers
just the words inside;
useless in France,
meaningless in America.

I've written nothing without your help.

For twenty years you've been my shadow bride,
calling me back to myself.
In every city of my escape
I've heard your voice.
In Paris we spoke our mother tongue
in each other's arms.
You wept for the familiar sounds.

When I was forty-three and met you for the first time
in Berlin, you cut my life in two.
I began again.
Today I'm sixty-eight years old on the docks of New York,
gulls swerving and wailing
above our broken faces.
We say goodbye for the first time.

Once you called at midnight
to talk about Hindemith,
to tell me how his overtones connect each bar,

invisible thread, sounds we can't hear.
These harmonics guide us through the music, resolve
the twelve tones like mist in a valley,
the reflection of sky in water,
the illusion that what's unnamed remains unformed.
Our voices connected by black wire,
words carried on waves.

We are the strain and stress of a line,
the poem's tension singing in each black wire
of words, and between the first line and the last.
We are the angle of light that burns water,
the point of intersection that creates perspective.

You have lived Brecht's parable of the Chalk Circle.
When I was caught in the middle, you let go
so I wouldn't be torn to pieces.
Your actions have taught me what it is to love—
that it's holding back, as well as holding.

For the first time I'm going
where you can't join me. I know that home
is the one place you won't come.
But you of all people must understand—
the need to hear my language in every mouth.
I can't think in America.

I've never let myself describe you
and now that there's no time left
your meaning spills out of me

like the essence of an atom cracking
on the edge of speed's bowl,
liquid in its longing to become part of something else,
transformed.

Flesh moves to become spirit.

You were the only one to understand my conversion.
Many people have asked me about God;
my proof is manifestation,
that God can be called
"getting over fear."

I wanted badly that truth be a single thing;
now I know it won't be measured.
It wasn't Heisenberg or Hindemith, but you
who convinced me
that nothing can be unravelled to its core,
that truth is a field, a cage, a cloud of sound.
How else to reconcile the faces of those running away
with the faces of those turning away,
with the faces of those in uniform—that hair-shirt
that says more about a man than his eyes
because you can't tell the parts of his face
that are his.
How else to encompass both that crying and those
orders; the sound of my own voice
begging, and my voice telling jokes to the man
without shoes beside me on a train;
how else to encompass the moon's chilling scream

as it calls out in its bad sleep above the earth
and your voice on the phone,
waking me in Paris, Los Angeles, New York.

How else to reconcile you
with my family;
our knowledge of each other
an invisible hypotenuse
connecting your marriage and mine.

You are like the church bells in Heidelberg:
walking through Philosopher's Way,
no sound of the city passes through the wall of trees
except the intermittent bells
calling me back to the place.

I've woken many nights
sweating from the same dream,
my body sprouting hands,
ripping from my sides with the pain
of broken bone parting skin.

Last night I looked out
to the grocer's across your street,
baskets of flowers lining the sidewalk,
trembling in the dark wind.
The gasp of paper and leaves
made me eighteen again—

nothing about the feeling had changed,
the ambush of longing October calls out.
I'm living proof
we don't stop wanting
what we can't have.

New York's a bad place to say goodbye,
but you're right—
it's no worse than any other.

For over twenty years
we've been joined: magician's hoops
caught and free, held together and apart
in desire and idea.

Like loons we travel underwater
great distances, to surface next to each other.
We burst up from water to air
to drift beside the serrated horizon of firs.

No matter where you are
or who you're near,
we come up for air together.

No matter my pace or distance,
it's you I surface to.

A Lesson from the Earth

*"God . . . began to play the game of signatures, signing His likeness
on to the world; therefore I chance to think that all nature and the
graceful sky are symbolized in the art of geometry."*

"Mine is the task of the mathematician."

—JOHANNES KEPLER

I begged scraps from the Rudolphine Table—
the rinds of orbits, stars scattering like pips spat
from Tycho's chewing mouth.
His servants hovered the meal, poured wine
into everyone's glass
but mine. I was angrier than an incomplete equation!
Until Tycho gave me Mars. A feast
of numbers. Starved so long,
my eyes were bigger than my belly;
I'll have the answer in eight days, I cried,
leaning into my plate. But it took eight years
to lick it, clean.

We were sent to each other, Tycho and I;
nothing is casually
causal: all motion the result of invisible force.
We were sent for a reason,
like curtains blown in from an open window
to knock over a cup.
Everything fell.
Even the beloved circles of planetary paths
spiralled down,
empty as a swirl of apple skin.
My Martian obsession: I was a dog
prowling the dark, stars stuck in my fur like burrs.

Tycho's house was a box of noise,
numbers shook in my head like seeds in a melon.
No escape from the stamping and shouting
of masons and cooks, the hunters home with dinner,
and above all, Tycho's interfering howls.
So I worked at night, straining to hear
the sacred chant of geometric love!
I sharpened my compasses on the window ledge
and felt the breeze of planets in their nightly procession;
all night I tramped the sky, wearied by gravity,
tidal forces pulled my hair! Naturally,
I slept in. At lunch
there was a sneer under Tycho's moustache,
a look to remind me he'd stayed up late
every night of his life. Tycho,
who'd even fought a duel in the dark
and forever after rubbed metal polish
where his nose used to be. Every servant had a joke
about tarnished cutlery.
A true nobleman, Tycho smelled of silver.
Sometimes, during the day, I hid outside,
my favourite place behind a pile of broken dishes
that seemed always shiny with blisters of rain;
or else any place quiet enough
for the effort of turning chaos
into cosmos.

Prague crumbled around us.
The Church turned its children against each other,
set fires in its own house.

Over the city smoke hung purple, ripped with sunlight;
ravens sewed up the sky with their black stitches.
An eleven-year-old girl prophesied the end of the world—
we had every reason to believe her.
Wounded shapes leaned against walls;
daughters and sons slipped between cannons and
through the fumes, to steal horse meat from the mud.
Amid all this—the problem
of Mars, god of war.
In the early hours I believed
only when I'd found the pattern of its orbit,
the hidden sense of it,
would the horrors end.

Priests point to sparrows, to rain,
to fruit falling from the trees,
in order to prove the earth stands still.
In the name of faith they only proclaim their doubt
by refusing to look through the telescope.
They say the truth is at stake; yes,
the truth seems nowhere else.
In Rome's Piazza dei Fiori
they burned Bruno, for believing in infinity.

We must learn at least this lesson from the earth,
that the greater must make room for the small,
just as the earth attracts even the smallest stone.
Just as the entire planetary system
rests on the plainest pattern.

As cathedrals replaced cross-beams and pillars
with a single arch,
so the Church must someday give up
hundreds of perfect circles,
for the simple, blasphemous ellipse.
In error begins truth.
I spent my life in dogged computation
to prove a sun-centred heaven. For years
my reasoning was a ball circling the curve of a hole,
but I believed I'd find an equation simple enough
to move the earth.
For twenty-two years I looked for ratios—
in sizes of the planets, in solar distances
and lengths of orbits—until God whispered:
measure not from the earth but from the sun.
And the heavens opened.

I know now why sailors sing.
The sea is so big it swallows geometry,
but not time.
Heaving and hauling with one voice,
they shift the sky on their backs.
So it is with the planets; dancing,
their skirts flare out behind them—
equal areas in equal time—
harmony of the spheres.

I used to think we escape time
by disappearing into beauty.

Now I see it's the opposite.
Beauty reveals time.

I saw my first eclipse when I was nine, above Emmendingen,
the moon rising from the clouds like an infant's head
in its web of blood; the last time
I held my father's hand.

Everything human and broken
depends on perfection.
Imperfect man, left unfinished
with the purpose of becoming whole.

A prisoner moon, I'm caught between papal earth and
Lutheran sun, heretic to both.
I've been pushed from Tübingen, Graz and Prague.
In Linz they took away my books
until Paul Guldin got them back—
he may be a Jesuit, but first
he's a mathematician.

They asked for me in every town; they'd be happy
with even false confession.

From Linz we travelled upriver
until the Danube froze, and I had to leave
Susannah and my daughters in Regensberg.
My head banged like a turnip against the back of the wagon
all the way to Ulm. But in my arms
the only copy of the Rudolphine Tables,

including a map of the world, a chronology of history, and
the positions of one thousand,
one hundred, and thirty-six stars.
Two lifetimes of devotion,
one spent bent over paper,
the other—Tycho alone in the dark,
his face red from leaning back, hand in his pocket
around a fist-sized globe of the sky
he carried with him since he was a boy.

Now Tycho's gone. His instruments—
the finest, none to match them anywhere—
rust in Tengnagel's cellar.
Gone, Tycho's Castle of the Stars,
the printing press and paper mill,
his forest, fish ponds and flower gardens,
his compass-makers and measurement-takers.

And Emperor Rudolph—gone;
with his imperial library and mechanical treasures,
the singing fountains and glass orchestras.

Tonight, arriving in Ulm,
I remembered a night as cold as this,
years ago, when the recognizable sky saved me
from the unrecognizable world.
From a bridge over the Moldau, all mystery poured up
and complex Prague fell away.
The sudden gift of the comet—
like a word mouthed, a sign,

a rock thrown across a lake without a sound—
and looking down, I saw the whole sky floating in the river:
"as above; so below."

Looking up again, I saw what has always been,
suspended since time began, for anyone to discover—
God's eternal clue:
the moon in its wet skin of light,
the moon not less in its halfness.

What I learned then sustains me
through every sorrow:
it's the believer who keeps looking for proof.

Modersohn–Becker

"There are many degrees of power in the world, and nowhere is the difference in degree greater than in the case of human will and human desire, just as water boils at one temperature, and molten iron at another."
—FYODOR DOSTOEVSKY

1

It did not free me to leave him.
All day at Worpswede rain stretches to the ground,
air like wood grain; burls of cloud.
Bark puckers on thin trees:
fingers too long in water.
By the end of the path, my sweater is beaded
with mist, a silver armour.
Where road wedges forest,
workhorses stagger like bodybuilders.
Snow is messy with spring, mud stains
under trees, like pools of shadow.
These are days when day doesn't arrive;
at night the same darkness falls into place.

I could smell pipe smoke in his hair.
Before I left,
in the peculiar quiet of a winter house,
windows startled dumb with ice—
we sat together on the stairs.
His head leaned on the banister.
Everyone said I was selfish.
Fear is selfish.

From Paris I wrote his name on a year of envelopes
until I finally saw

the shape of it: Otto—two bodies, two mouths.
The gutter ran with lights
and in the empty street I heard our loneliness
in a dog's throat.

Every way into myself
fills up with blood.

The joy that's close to terror; colour,
the hot pulse that hurts through veins.

In this light his eyes are clotted with oil.
The studio smells of wood smoke.
The birds ask their same questions.

My hands are stained with his face.

2

In 1900, Cézanne's paintings were stacked against a wall
in Vollard's basement. I couldn't believe
those secret squares of colour, fermenting in the dark,
unrecognized.
Paris wasn't the same after that.
And watching Rodin shape thought,
like a blind man learning a face,
I saw what it means to merge with work.
Rodin, who felt the sculptor Clara could become,
cut away the excess.
My friend emerged in his hands.

Watching him gather hair like flowing water
from a stone scalp,
pulling the face open
into love—
breasts like leaves dripping with rain,
legs taut as roots—
I suddenly understood that painting too
never lets you escape
awareness of the human hand:
the source of light
is the painter's body.

I thought that finding my own hot centre
would teach me colour.
Clara circled her clay while I stared so long at the canvas
I was dragged under.
Even the spirit has limits,
humility rising like silence,
the silence of light, gold rising from the fields.

    •

We left Paris, the Pont des Arts
still lined with violets.
At Worpswede, the hills burned under September's glass.
Clara and I wore white to soak up the last light,
like bread the last bit of soup.

We first saw Rilke pushing furniture
through a doorway. I named the scene:
Struggle, With A Table;
later learned the truth of it.

By the fire, listening to a chamber concert,
the kind of music where loss wears gloves.
Rilke's eyes were on us.
That night he said things like "let me stay in the storm!"
and "give me autumn!"
Everyone was aware of him.

He followed me outside;
we washed our faces in the cold air.

.

What was missing in me, Rilke knew.

Nights together, midnight tea
in my studio, where, he said,
"everything becomes mysterious."

He talked about Tolstoy, and how we must earn
death. From Rilke you can learn about love
just watching him hold a cup or peel an orange.

Black roofs bled through thin snow,
words on a page. At the window, our legs
long against each other, grass in a current.

But his kind of love deepens
only with loss. He smells what's burning
better than what's fresh.
Rilke, don't be a "writer," stay
a man who writes!

"What do you know about it, Paula?"

That's how it was. To him, I was Paula.
But he was always "Rilke."

.

Skating on the Christmas pond;
lamps like owls in the trees.
I crushed fans of spruce and buried my face in my hands
as if in a book. While Rilke read inside,
his beautiful head bent from his body
like a stem "broken" by the line of water in a vase.

He married Clara and soon she was moving horizontally,
a figurehead on a ship, pregnant with their daughter.
His invisible barrier between them;
birds hitting glass.

.

Married, my aesthetic turned physical,
a knowledge I couldn't paint:
a heap of coltsfoot,
its yellow points curling on the table;
the white bedroom of birches, our faces cold,
the warmth of us under clothes—sometimes
chocolate, a blanket—until darkness
rolled on top of the light, leaving only
the small breathing spaces of stars.
The accidental beauty
of things brought in from outside,

leaves and crushed mignonettes carried in on sweaters:
the unplanned life that purled our days.
Following his trail: chair still rocking, lit pipe,
the apple changing colour on the plate.

Only love sees the familiar for the first time.

The light changing Otto's face, changing
him.
Winter turning the walls blue.
Imagining him naked, even as he stood there,
naked.

    •

Opened by hills;
unnerving metal yellow of birch leaves
between my teeth;
forest's green chill on my shoulders.
Ice filled my veins,
the pond the colour of drowned ghosts, ragged as a shadow.
Trees pushed up through my throat,
leaves crowded my eyes and
I looked. Grateful, bursting with shape and colour.
I held my husband until I felt his face inside my own,
until my skin was blind with attention—
and still I didn't know anything, still
my hand was stupid.
My eyes went black, I held the brush,
choking on a thread of song.

    •

I started again; where everything starts:
at the body. Classes in life-drawing,
training my hand to see.

In Paris alone,
my family waiting for me to give up
so I could go back to being "happy."

Every day, failure boiled up into my throat
and stayed there.

.

Obsession is the sacrifice of light
to the richness of submergence.
But love is separation,
the membrane of the orange dividing itself,
the surface of silver
that turns glass into a mirror.

There's failure in every choice.

Art emerges from silence;
silence, from one's place in the world.

.

Not that paint captures light,
but that light breaks free from the paint.

I imagined autumn in Worpswede, the tangled red
wire of empty bushes, a ceramic sky

crazed with branches. I sank deep in myself,
breathing in as if my bones were cedar.

Nowhere have I felt closer to love
than there, alone in that city.

Stars are flickering tips of snakes;
starlight, their fragile skin cast behind.

My dreams longed for Otto, for forest, for home.
I woke and the space was empty, except for paintings:
my step-daughter playing recorder,
hollow vowels slipping through the trees,
streaming behind her;
my sister's black hair pulled tight,
sleek as a mink, her braid a watery tail down her back.

Then I felt crazy—my two lives, simultaneous.

Two whites: snow on the birches.

•

Fulfilment is wordless,
the silence when skin takes over.

But when you're not speaking with skin,
you must love with language.

Rilke would say that's even more intimate—
the instant words become picture,
leaping from his throat, to my inner eye.

.

The first spring day, with Otto in the garden.

My mother crossed the grass, her arms open,
like a child waiting to be lifted.
Since five in the morning she'd travelled towards me.

We pulled the table out to the verandah,
set the blue dishes.
My dress round as the billowing cloth.

3

Branches dip, dripping.
Rain gets in everywhere, its animated shadow
fills every surface.
Dreams that usually evaporate in the light
stay wet with darkness.

That I'm looking for something I can't find
makes me strangely satisfied.
It fills me with time.

All my life I've been saying grace
for hunger: invisible, smelling of earth,
heavy as cattle down a darkening field,
their bodies pushing their heads close to the ground,
their necklaces of bells.

.

Every painting is a way of saying goodbye.

Flowers

There's another skin inside my skin
that gathers to your touch, a lake to the light;
that looses its memory, its lost language
into your tongue,
erasing me into newness.

Just when the body thinks it knows
the ways of knowing itself,
this second skin continues to answer.

In the street—café chairs abandoned
on terraces, market stalls emptied
of their solid light,
though pavement still breathes
summer grapes and peaches.
Like the light of anything that grows
from this newly turned earth,
every tip of me gathers under your touch,
wind wrapping my dress around our legs,
your shirt twisting to flowers in my fists.

Anniversary

Tonight a Buick's our bedroom,
cold wind off the lake muffled by closed windows.
Thirty years ago we drove through dark mountains
on a narrow road, as if under blankets with a flashlight.
Three days and two nights to the sea,
past grain elevators leaning against the horizon
like the heads on Easter Island;
under stars like ibises
swooping through mangroves.
Thirty years from our wedding and still
we're sleeping in cars. Still
awake as the moon, foreheads burning.

Fresh Mint

Fresh mint slinks towards us through the dark kitchen,
crowds the table,
loud with its own good suggestions.

Persuasive as an extra electron, it changes
conversation, reminds us of
something. Insidious.
The way there's always
more glasses than guests at the end of a meal.

It binds us in its loose weave,
thread of moonlight in water.

Soon we don't notice
the wild smell,
being so filled with it.

Phantom Limbs

"The face of the city changes more quickly, alas! than the mortal heart."
—CHARLES BAUDELAIRE

So much of the city
is our bodies. Places in us
old light still slants through to.
Places that no longer exist but are full of feeling,
like phantom limbs.

Even the city carries ruins in its heart.
Longs to be touched in places
only it remembers.

Through the yellow hooves
of the ginkgo, parchment light;
in that apartment where I first
touched your shoulders under your sweater,
that October afternoon you left keys
in the fridge, milk on the table.
The yard—our moonlight motel—
where we slept summer's hottest nights,
on grass so cold it felt wet.
Behind us, freight trains crossed the city,
a steel banner, a noisy wall.
Now the hollow diad
floats behind glass
in office towers also haunted
by our voices.

Few buildings, few lives
are built so well
even their ruins are beautiful.
But we loved the abandoned distillery:
stone floors cracking under empty vats,
wooden floors half rotted into dirt,
stairs leading nowhere, high rooms
run through with swords of dusty light.
A place the rain still loved, its silver paint
on rusted things that had stopped moving it seemed, for us.
Closed rooms open only to weather,
pungent with soot and molasses,
scent-stung. A place
where everything too big to take apart
had been left behind.

Pillar of Fire

At Katimbang, dead birds rained out of the sky.
Statues walked.

Whole forests—strewn like driftwood.
Tides so fast, fish were stranded,
then picked from the ground like a crop.

Father, I remember when we first
sailed through together—
how simple fear was, then.
Docked at Merak you told the story
of Sunda ghost, a sailor
who paid for the sins of this life
in the next, by having to gather
all the islands in the Strait.
The lights of port behind you;
breeze snapping the ropes:
"at night you'll hear him howling,
his hands full and his work half done."
My hair jumped when I first heard the sound.
You kept me scared. Then told me
about orangutans, who'll howl like babies
when the weather's shifting.
Now I can tell you,
Sunda Strait is surely haunted.

Our destination was Hong Kong,
carrying cargo from Belfast.
As usual, the first day we pull from shore,
each man was busy with his own thoughts.

And as usual, Willy—John's son—was below,
sleeping off his leave;
he never came aboard on his own legs.

At first it sounded like cannon fire, a distress;
but not a ship in sight.
The threat of damnation isn't always
something you can see.
Then a line of weather covered half the sky.
I shortened sail, turned southwest to face the wind.

Like meteors, like white comets chained with flame,
the pumice fell—stones bigger than a man's head,
the size of pumpkins—
then smaller ones, almost worse
because they came so fast; in seconds
we were deep in ash.

The sea was a swaying field of pumice,
frozen foam.
And then—a jungle floated towards us,
palms standing straight up;
as if we sailed through dry land.

Midnight, suffocating
on a sea that looked like dirty ice.
Choked with sulphur,
eyes burning into our heads.
Cinders everywhere, the air itself was on fire.
The sea boiled.

Father, at thirty fathoms,
the lead came up hot!
Mastheads and yardarms—lined with spark.

By morning, the strait was clear.
We even laughed when Willy,
who'd slept through it all,
came up for watch and wouldn't believe a word.

But then we saw the lighthouse at Fourth Point
snap like a stem.

And day was night,
land was sea,
the earth fell out of the sky.

Noon, and we were in a darkness we could feel.
Burning mud, glowing green and blue,
slapped the deck—
the sound that hits a coffin.
We shouted constantly, because we couldn't see;
and dug, for fear of sinking under the weight.
I called for the sidelights
and sent the two Jameses forward.
The mate and second in either quarter,
and someone to keep mud off the binnacle glass—
though we were blind as the dead.

Lightning lit our faces,
ugly with work.
The air—smeared solid.

When it stopped
we fell where we stood, as if we'd had only
the exact amount of strength.

The dark was full of stories,
of names of wives and children;
stories that, when light returned,
would never be spoken again.

It lightened enough to see the horizon.
Our first sight of land was West Island.

A mist of sand began to fall.
Krakatoa roared, ear-aching loud,
though we were a full seventy-five miles away.
The *Charles Bal*—from truck to waterline,
spars, sails, and ropes—
hard with mud;
as if she'd been raised from the bottom.

A miracle, not a man hurt.
But—in Anjer, Merak,
all the villages of the Java Coast!

Father, the places you stopped so often
for water and wood, meat and fruit
have vanished.

They say that when the blast came,
in the streets of Katimbang
mud galloped fast as horses;

that burning ash pushed through floors
like pillows bursting their stuffing.
They say that when people ran through the streets
they left red footprints of fire.
That their bare arms looked like torn sleeves.

We knew them.

They say that even now, even far as Ceylon,
when you cut open fish
you find jewellery that belonged to the dead.

The town of Tjiringin is now ocean.

Blue Vigour

I think, if you have lived through a war
or have made your home in a country
not your own, or if you've learned
to love one man,
then your life is a story.

Eight thousand feet above the sea's devotions
sail the four Ngong hills.
The East Wind—"King Solomon's favourite horse"—
rides over the plain to the foothills;
you follow the monsoon's path to my farm,
desert in your clothes and hair.

If you love a man who's not your husband,
your life becomes the story everyone else tells.

For months we were still as animals
alert to an enemy. We stalked each other with the charged
passivity of the inevitable.
With the patience and impatience of obsession.

I learned about you
the way I learned about the river
at the edge of my farm—
I can't see it from the house,
but know its path by the acacias
that grow along it.

What I couldn't foresee
led me to you.

During the act of greatest trust
my husband gave me a lasting gift.
I was rotten with his *mal d'amour;*
they had to send me home.
Almost thirty, back in my mother's house.
When I could walk again, her narrow arm
steered me through the garden,
green peony hands glistening
like the acres of coffee I'd left behind.
I leaned against her,
missing her youth as well as my own.
Home, yet not home.
Although the marriage was over,
I had the farm.
Although we hadn't yet touched,
I longed for Ngong and your body.

Sleepless on the boat
I pressed against the railing,
leaned into my future.
To deny another's happiness
by denying your own—
that could only be an adult misery.

I know your value
because you give yourself
just as you're leaving.
Each sojourn refines our feeling—
together we are stones tumbling to jewels,

beans polishing in the coffee-dryer,
gleaming under the lanterns.

When we stayed at your house
on the Takaunga, the moon was firm
in the shaking sky.
We were alive as coral pools,
where water shapes the rock
and rock shapes water.

Each time you return
you ask for another story.
Your expectation lets me love you
when you're gone.
My wanting would have both encased me
and driven me out of my skin
like an insect under the canopy at night—
were it not for words.
Each day I write to greet you.

Those mornings when one side of my bed
is cool with your absence,
I rise to the window and loving you,
the Ngong hills gather me in.

With each parting
my heart is forced to grow,
because the only way to love you
is to love each particle of green and

each animal part of life—
muscle, skin, and bone—
that dots and darts and hides
in the view from my room.

And now that you've learned to fly,
and really ride King Solomon's East Wind,
I have to love the air.

On the Terrace

They say the brush is strapped to my hand—
it's not true.
My palms fold in and Gabrielle wraps them,
in powdered gauze, to stop the chafing.
In fact, the brush fits nicely in that crevice,
my fingers like vines around a trunk.
Sometimes it startles me;
my twisted joints, the brush so straight.

All morning, sweating over the olives—
those leaves use every colour for grey.
Years ago, when I stopped working outside—
what a commotion
because a man came in out of the rain.
Raphael didn't have to drag his canvas through fields
in order to paint sunlight.
I was tired; every time I looked up
the light was somewhere else.
Clouds, the wind, made a sleeve change colour or
leaves turn over their other green.
It's lonely, letting the world wash over you.
Those days, everyone looked away. In love;
or drinking, heads leaned back,
eyes focused on the bottom of a glass.
But now I'm kept company.
Women look me in the eye when I take their clothes off.
I'm a fine son of a tailor, painting nudes!
Gabrielle gains twenty pounds under my brush.

When I was young, I wanted to move with the world,
didn't realize the world moves in us.
A still life isn't about fruit, but about
time.

And there's a stillness inside things
as they move; think of waterlilies—
Poor Monet, his blind eyes filled with water!
The lilies float in his mind.

That's why I can't agree with Zola—
so concerned to describe the surface,
he forgets the spaces between things,
forgets that touching isn't holding.
Too busy with "iridescence" and "shimmering,"
he forgets to say it's raining.
It was my mistake too, forgetting space.
When I was a student of the Seine
with Monet at Bougival,
we learned how colours vibrate.
But space vibrates too.
That's what musicians know.
If Zola were here, he'd sit in that chair,
eyes burning everything in sight—
convinced that's the way to see—
and in the end, like all the others,
he'd deduce:
the brush is strapped to my hand.

Stillness in motion. I illustrate my point.
They carry me like a king from one room to another;
when I shout,
they rush to pick the brush hairs from the paint.

And now that I have no hands,
I long for clay.
Why begin sculpture now?
Riviere's the only one who'd ask.
I couldn't tell him
it was because of a dream,
that I'd slept back, thirty years,
to *The Bathers* at Versailles.

Girardon himself had become limestone;
he looked so happy there, among them.
Now I want a woman
who'll wait for me in a garden,
in any weather, every light.

In the afternoons I watch them work the stone.
One day, without lifting a hand,
the form in my head
will be exactly what I see.

Stone

Beatrice called him a pig and a pearl.
But she also liked to say,
lovers are equal only when so steeped
in corruption, knowledge of the other
is no longer a weapon.

Modi was a fallen king,
royalty in trousers held up with rope,
quoting Dante and Petrarch on park benches.
Cocaine and absinthe made him
play the naked bull in the street.
I've heard all the stories from everyone
who never knew him.
Modi wandering the halls, ripping wallpaper,
gouging at plaster until his nails bled—
because he was drunk. No. Because
he wanted to get at brick,
to feel stone under his fingers.
At night he used to steal
blocks from construction sites, until
the war, when no one was building any more.
He resented his own walls,
hundreds of stone women surrounding him,
unreachable.

He was close to Rivera
and painted him as a balloon;
Diego will never get stuck, he said,
Diego's free.

His old self clung to him,
an open mouth on his sleeve; a shadow
that turned him around in the street,
or in his sleep. His last nights were spent
with a stranger, the Greek, who knew nothing
of his failures, but knew
the Mediterranean.
He drank himself back to where he was born.

There are two kinds of spiritual biography:
Modi stuffed his soul with life.
I starved for the sake of my soul.

At first it wasn't passion, felt more
like memory—as if, in remaining true to myself,
to everything in my life that had come before,
there could be no direction but towards him.

We even met in an old embrace.
Modi was alone in Nice,
months after we'd been introduced,
when suddenly he knew me.
He came back to Montmartre. For weeks
we walked the city, resting in a cinema
or crémerie and he never stopped talking.
His baroque attentions, his rococo tongue!
The whole city in his face.
We drank to his *cara Italia*, his mother,
to Giovanna who he'd never see grown;

but he stayed sober and no hashish,
which he used to take like dinner mints
after meals at Rosalie's or the Rotonde.

He accepted beauty wherever it was offered,
black iron fences against the snow,
bare trees smeared like charcoal on a wet sky.

We sat together at dozens of tables,
so poised for love, if I moved an inch
I would've caught one wing in the sea
and toppled, squawking, water-logged,
everything spoiled by closeness.
Faith turned to hunger
like a sweater pulled inside out, over my head.

Our walks transformed Paris: desire
clinging like windy paper to legs;
sharp as gasoline and leather polish, wet wool and
Modi's scent in my coat;
hopeless as the horses patrolling a vanished city,
pulling beans and potatoes in crowded streets.

The higher the ledge of his art,
the more the world pulled at his feet.

It wasn't only his lungs not strong enough.
The last trip home, he showed photos of his heads.

His friends brayed and barked, begged him
to put the stone out of its misery,
to smash it back into pavement.
He spent months on a single carving.
Five or six years
of happiness, nights when he lit candles and
embraced the day's work, a pagan.
Later he endured the portraits abused too—
as a roof for rabbits, as walls for a chicken coop—
by Libion and the butcher who took them
in exchange for cheese and eggs.
Nobody tells that part of the story.
When he was dead and worth ten times his life,
of course they tried to sell them.
But the canvases were too damaged.

No one cares about Modi now, another painter
from an old avant garde,
a man whose faces have been cut
into postcards, puzzles, ashtrays.

Only limestone loved him perfectly,
resisted with integrity, showed him
what to do. Demanded slowness, will,
mistakes not easy to fix.
But paint submitted to frenzy.
He was powerful. His love
was less.

His great dream—to sculpt a temple of women,
the "pillars of tenderness" he believed
held up the world.
Instead—his nudes. Outside of time and place;
no fruit, no flowers or furniture,
just the glowing body,
the certainty of pleasure.
A scandal—
to paint the body no longer anonymous:
each woman with a different knowledge.
It was Picasso's work that was immoral—
he tore off the woman's clothes then
tore apart the woman.
Modi's models simply . . . disrobed.

He wasn't a cubist, because he believed
if you break the bowl you can't describe
what's in the bowl;
destroy a shape—its spirit dissipates.
He was only a cubist when it came to love.

His portraits—every face a eulogy to stone
but without its calm.
The concentration of a last glance or
an approach;
as if, as he held them in his gaze,
they were already melting away.
He believed it was better to burn with time,

to match its speed with your own,
like the moment you can follow rain with your eyes.

When he painted,
he found you.
Beatrice was fire, Jeanne was nectar,
I was clear water, affected by the slightest touch.
He focused on my throat, that long river between
brain and body, between what you say and
what you give. The line of my neck
graceful, elegant as the handle of a pitcher.
My face flushed under its whiteness,
so covered with his touch, yet
so untouched, so—tragic!

Jeanne looked like a gypsy, with her violin.
But all she knew was Bach.
Her devotion was a fugue,
he got tangled up in himself, trying to leave her.
He did everything to push her away;
she did nothing but remain still.

He judged her gently,
painted every weakness, her double chin,
but the whole story came out on canvas,
everything she was thinking:
how Modi looked at four in the morning,
how he slept, close, without forgetting her.

Jeanne was a woman who could look at one face forever,
if she knew how the arms held.

When he died, she jumped,
big with Modi's life.
I feel certain it was a son.

No one believed in him, not even Jeanne,
who in the end, believed only in his body.

A few years ago
on a train to London, a man
brought Modi back to me.
He was Welsh and lived in a place so set aside
it was like the detail of a painting.
I liked him right away; when he sat down he said,
pardon me if I smell of horses.
He'd walked through fields to reach the station.

Half his life in Africa, and now
he spent his days drawing farm animals
in a motel room by the sea.
We talked our way across England;
he said, I belong nowhere, half here,
half there.
I'd give anything to see this place
as I used to—when I was young.
When my life was still imagined.

We passed fields smoky with rain
hay lying loose, flat as wet hair.

The glass was ghostly bark, wrinkled with water
and it was like looking out a café window—
I'm an old woman but I could smell wet wool,
horses, the sweet brown breath of coffee.

The Welshman said,
some people regret not what they've done
but what they haven't, and then decide:
this is my life. No;
you've missed your life.
But even the truth can't change the past.
When you're old, time is like a toothache,
still—you're happy to have teeth in your mouth.
Pardon me if I've upset you.

Better to let the past dissolve in you,
grow small; still as
smell.

I love horses, the man said,
they're the most noble of animals.
They're beautiful even while they're working.
It's the *Iliad*, isn't it—
where even the horses weep on the bloody field.

It was cold, late afternoon, the room was dark—
Paris winter—but the window
was a painting, thick with light.
Modi's arms around my waist.
He told me that in Cagnes
the light was so bright it drove him crazy,

so he and Soutine stepped into a barn;
it was cool and dark
and suddenly he felt the warm
breath of a horse on his hair.

Our gratitudes were heaped against the day.
In the dimness, the room was a garden,
silk waterfalls of robes down the closet door and
flowing from sill to floor.

Keep everything you can't.

III

What the Light Teaches

"I break open stars and find nothing and again nothing,
and then a word in a foreign tongue."

—ELISABETH BORCHER

1

Countless times this river has been bruised by our bodies;
liquid fossils of light.

We shed our ghost skins in the current;
then climb the bank, heavy and human.

The river is a loose tongue,
a folk song. At night we go down to listen.
Stars like sparks from a bonfire.
We take off what we are,
and step into the moon.

2

When there are no places left for us,
this is where we'll still meet.
Past the white fountain of birches,
green helmets of willows.
Past the boulder that fastens the field
like a button on a pocket.
Here, where trees you planted are now twice our height.

In winter we'll haunt your kitchen, our love
an overturned bowl, a circling lid.

We'll visit the creaking bog with its sunken masts;
fly over a death mask of snow
and the frozen pond striped with grass—
to our river, humming between closed lips.
Attentive as your favourite poet,
Tsvetaeva—who listened with the roots of her hair.

3

Birds plunge their cries like needles
into the thick arm of afternoon.

Beyond the closed window, soundless pines—
a heavy green brocade; and the glowing, stiff
brushcut of the corn.
Wands of wild calla.
Lilies tall as children.

You're asleep on the couch, head up, as if in a bath;
summer heat turns thin white sleeves
pink against your skin.
Sleeping as if you'd waited years
for a place to close your eyes.

Everything familiar:
dishes and smells, faces in oval wooden frames,
tins of Russian tea
with their forest scenes, their borders of black and gold,
lining the shelves.

We float in death,
the ordinary world holds together
like the surface tension of water,
still and stretched, a splash of light.
The shadow pattern of leaves,
a moving tattoo on your bare legs.

4

Sometimes I was afraid to touch him,
afraid my hand would go right through him.
But he was alive, in a history
made more painful by love.

I prayed to the sky to lift our father's head,
to deliver him from memory.

I wished he could lie down
in music he knew intimately, and become
sound, his brain flooded by melody so powerful
it would stretch molecules, dismantle thought.

5

Suspended in flux, in contortions of disorder,
in the frozen acrobatics of folding and faults,
the earth mourns itself.
Continents torn in half and turned into coastlines,
call for themselves across the sea.

Caves, frantic for air, pull themselves up
by the ground, fields collapsing into empty sockets.
Everywhere the past juts into the present;
mountains burst from one era to another,
or crumple up millennia, time joining at its ends.

We also pleat time.
Remembering, we learn to forget.
The kind of forgetting that stops us, one foot
in the spring soil of your farm,
the other in mud where bits of bone and teeth
are still suspended, a white alphabet.
The kind of forgetting that changes
moonlight on the river into shreds of skin.
The forgetting that is the heart's
filthy drain,
so fear won't overflow its deep basin.

Even in its own confusion,
in its upheavals and depressions,
the earth has room in its heart.
Carefully, part by part, it replaces us.
Gently, so bones may embrace a little longer,
mud replaces marrow.

The dogs slip like mercury through the long grass.

How can we but feel they're here,
in the strange darkness of a thermosensitive sky,
even as light gushes over rocks
and the sun drips sweet fat the colour of peaches

over fields. Here, in the noise of the river,
a mother gives birth in a sewer;
soldiers push sand down a boy's throat.

Theirs are voices we hear
but can't hear, like the silence
of parents rounded up in a town square,
who stopped their tongues in time,
saving children by not
calling out to them in the street.

Our father's daughters, we can't dream ourselves
into another world, see things differently.
Instead, we try to withstand memory
with memory, to go back further, to before:
back to the dacha in the high forests of Kochtobel,
to the Moyka in our mother's silvery photo of Petersburg,
to the wooden sidewalks of Kiev.
You read poems in the old language
even our parents can't speak—
what we save, saves us—
and in your mouth the soft buzzes are natural as cicadas,
the long "ayas" like bird calls.

Language is how ghosts enter the world.
They twist into awkward positions
to squeeze through the black spaces.
The dead read backwards,
as in a mirror. They gather

in the white field and look up,
waiting for someone
to write their names.

Language remembers.
Out of obscurity, a word takes its place
in history. Even a word so simple
it's translatable: number. Oven.

Because all change is permanent,
we need words to raise ourselves
to new meaning: tea and dacha and river.

6

It stopped me, the first time
I looked out at our father in the yard and saw
how she leaned her head on his shoulder—
familiar, and full of desire.

Together they looked at a nest in the bushes,
inspected strawberries.
Although the air was humid with lilacs,
heavy with insects and rain,
she was cool in a dress the colour of the moon.

You were reading by the open door.
The sound of a lawn mower made everything still.

Then a moment like night cereus
that blooms only in the dark, waking us
with its alarm of scent.

It wasn't seeing your face so suddenly like his,
or the sight of death in her white dress;
or the glaze of summer light
hardening into crust. Not the accustomed sadness
of what we'd lost,
but a new injury, a gash
bleeding into everything:
what we were losing.

7

When there are no places left for us,
we'll still talk in order to make things true:
not only the years before we were born,
not only the names of our dead,
but also this life.
The simple feel of an apple in the hand.
The look of the table after a meal, *en déshabillé*,
rings of wine like lips staining the cloth,
the half-eaten fish in its halo of lemon and butter.
Nights of tastes, of different smoothnesses;
nights when the twister of desire touches down
and tears up sleep;
of drowning in the shadow of your own body.

But if memory is only skin,
if we become dervishes spinning
at the speed of the world, feeling
nothing,
we spend hours by the river, telling everything.
So that when we are gone, even our spirits
weighed down with stones,
the river will remember.

8

It was a suicide mission, to smuggle language
from mouths of the dying
and the dead; last words of the murdered mothers—
Germany, Poland, Russia.
They found that what they'd rescued
wasn't the old language at all;
only the alphabet the same.
Because language of a victim only reveals
the one who named him.

Because they were plucked from the centre,
because they shared the same table, same street,
there was no idiom to retreat to.

What was left but to cut out one's tongue,
or cleave it with new language,
or try to hear a language of the dead,

who were thrown into pits, into lakes—
What are the words for earth, for water?

The truth is why words fail.
We can only reveal by outline,
by circling absence.
But that's why language
can remember truth when it's not spoken.
Words in us that deafen,
that wait, even when their spell seems
wasted;
even while silence
accumulates to fate.

Prayer is the effort of wresting words
not from silence,
but from the noise of other words.
To penetrate heaven, we must reach
what breaks in us.
The image haunts me:
the double swaying
of prayer on the trains.

9

Whole cities were razed with a word.
Petersburg vanished into Leningrad, became
an invisible city where poets promised to meet

so they could pronounce again
"the blessed word with no meaning."

A writer buried his testimony
in the garden, black type in black soil,
trusting that someday earth would speak.
All those years of war and uncertainty after,
no one knew the power of his incantation,
calling quietly from its dark envelope.
From his notebook grew orchids and weeds.

Words are powerless as love,
transforming only by taking us as we are.

Reading letters from Tsvetaeva to a friend
we cried together in your barn:
"you're the only one I have left."

After all these years I still feel closest to you
in the hours reserved for nightmares,
even in our distant bedrooms.
Because I know you're awake too,
if not this night, then another,
watching your husband's sleeping body
rise with breath.

10

For years I've driven towards you in spring rain,
storm sky of green marble,
slow traffic a caravan of swinging lanterns,
windshield wipers like clock hands.
Poems by Tsvetaeva on the seat beside me,
flowers in wet paper.

As the hours pass, the hard seeds in my heart
soften and swell as I think of your kitchen
with its stone floor
like a summerhouse in Peredelkino,
and of Mandelstam, exiled to Yelabuga on the Kama:
"if you must leave the city,
it's best to live near a river."

You fly out of the darkness at me,
twisting open the tin sky.

The thunderstorm becomes other storms:
darkness steeping like tea above Burnside Drive,
with its slippery crease of rusted leaves;
or the night on High Street, rain
streaming like milk down the windshield
the moment the streetlights clicked on.
I think of young Akhmatova,
under a black umbrella with Modigliani,

reading Verlaine in the Luxembourg.
All the languages they spoke—
Russian, Italian, French—
and still, their lovemaking was with roses!
Language not enough
for what they had to tell each other.

Never to lose this joy,
driving to one who awaits my arrival.

Soon I will be standing on your porch, dripping
with new memory, a thin dress soaked with May rain.

Rain that helps one past grow out of another.

11

Language is the house with lamplight in its windows,
visible across fields. Approaching, you can hear
music; closer, smell
soup, bay leaves, bread—a meal for anyone
who has only his tongue left.
It's a country; home; family:
abandoned; burned down; whole lines dead, unmarried.
For those who can't read their way in the streets,

or in the gestures and faces of strangers,
language is the house to run to;
in wild nights, chased by dogs and other sounds,
when you've been lost a long time,
when you have no other place.

There are nights in the forest of words
when I panic, every step into thicker darkness,
the only way out to write myself into a clearing,
which is silence.
Nights in the forest of words
when I'm afraid we won't hear each other
over clattering branches, over
both our voices calling.

In winter, in the hour
when the sun runs liquid then freezes,
caught in the mantilla of empty trees;
when my heart listens
through the cold stethoscope of fear,
your voice in my head reminds me
what the light teaches.
Slowly you translate fear into love,
the way the moon's blood is the sea.

Skin Divers

I

Three Weeks

Three weeks longing, water burning
stone. Three weeks leopard blood
pacing under the loud insomnia of stars.
Three weeks voltaic. Weeks of winter
afternoons, darkness half descended.
Howling at distance, ocean
pulling between us, bending time.
Three weeks finding you in me in new places,
luminescent as a tetra in depths,
its neon trail.
Three weeks shipwrecked on this mad island;
twisting aurora of perfumes. Every boundary of body
electrified, every thought hunted down
by memory of touch. Three weeks of open eyes
when you call, your first question,
Did I wake you . . .

Skin Divers

Under the big-top
of stars, cows drift
from enclosures, bellies brushing
the high grass, ready for their heavy
festivities. Lowland gleams like mica
in the rain. Starlight
soaks our shoes.
The seaweed field begs, the same
burlap field that in winter cracks with frost,
is splashed by the black brush
of crows. Frozen sparklers of Queen Anne's lace.

Because the moon feels loved, she lets our eyes
follow her across the field, stepping
from her clothes, strewn silk
glinting in furrows. Feeling loved, the moon loves
to be looked at, swimming
all night across the river.

She calls through screens,
she fingers a white slip in the night hallway,
reaches across the table for a glass.
She holds the dream fort.
Like the moon, I want to touch places
just by looking. To tell
new things at three in the morning, when we're
awake with rain or any sadness, or slendering through
reeds of sleep, surfacing to skin. In this room
where so much has happened, where love
is the clink of buttons as your shirt slides

to the floor, the rolling sound of loose change;
a book half open, clothes
half open. Again we feel
how transparent the envelope
of the body, pushed through the door
of the world. To read what's inside
we hold each other
up to the light. We hold
the ones we love or long
to be free of, carry them
into every night field, sit with them
while cows slow as ships
barely move in the distance.
Rain dripping from the awning of stars.

Waterworn, the body remembers
like a floodplain, sentiment-laden,
reclaims itself with every tide.
Memory terraces, soft as green deltas.
Or reefs and cordilleras—
gathering the world to bone.

The moon touches everything
into meaning, under her blind fingers,
then returns us to cerulean
aluminum dawns. Night,
a road pointing east.
Her sister, memory, browses the closet
for clothes carrying someone's shape.
She wipes her hands on an apron

stained with childhood, familiar smells
in her hair; rattles pots and pans
in the circadian kitchen.
While in the bedroom of a night field,
the moon undresses; her abandoned peignoir
floats forever down.

Memory drags possessions out on the lawn,
moves slowly through wet grass, weighed down
by moments caught in her night net, in the glistening
ether of her skirt. The air alive,
memory lifts her head and I nearly
disappear. You lift your head, a look I feel
everywhere, a tongue of a glance,
and love's this dark field, our shadow web
of voices, the carbon-paper purple
rainy dark. Memory's heavy with the jewellery
of rain, her skirt heavy with buds of mercury
congealing to ice on embroidered branches—
as she walks we hear the clacking surf
of those beautiful bones. Already love
so far beyond the body, reached only
by way of the body. Time is the alembic
that turns what we know
into mystery. Into air,
into the purple stain of sweetness.
Laburnum, wild iris, birch forest so thick
it glows at night, smells that reach us
everywhere; the alchemy that keeps us
happy on the ground, even if our arms embrace

nothing, nothing: the withdrawing
trochee of birds. We'll never achieve escape
velocity, might as well sink into wet
firmament, learn to stay under,
breathing through our skin.
In silver lamella, in rivers
the colour of rain. Under water, under sky;
with transparent ancient wings.

Tonight the moon traipses in bare feet,
silk stockings left behind
like pieces of river.

Our legs and arms, summer-steeped,
slapped damp
with mud and weeds.

We roll over the edge into the deep field,
rise from under rain,
from our shapes in wet grass.
Night swimmers, skin divers.

Land in Sight

All day the sky
whispered into the sea and the sails
would not fill. On the pier,
dogs drank the air dry
with searching tongues.
We were seared wherever clothes
revealed us. Down the boulevard,
shutters clapped loud against the sun.
Children slipped messages through the slats,
flecks of paper drifted into the street.

All through the city love looked for us, through
the crooked *Altestrasse,* under Lenin's balcony,
past the terrace where Goethe drank his coffee.
Into cafés where coolness turns its key
in a shadow. All day love followed us
as we climbed, from fountain to bridge.
A gull hovered as if
broken. All day love drew its finger
across my belly, ascended my damp spine.
I kept turning my face
from its breath.

The city woke. Dogs unfolded their legs
and stood. One by one, shutters parted,
glimpses of voices
pressed the air.

The same loneliness that closes us
opens us again.

Like hair loosened by the sea,
slowly the darkness opens into darkness.

Night Garden

Your mouth, a hand
against my mouth.
Pressed to earth, we dream
of ocean: heat-soaked, washed
with exhaustion, our mariner's sleep
haunted by smells of garden—fresh rosemary
thirty miles off Spain. Long grasses
sway the bottom of our boat.
We follow a sequence
of scents complex as music,
navigate earth places, sea places, follow
acoustics of mountains,
warbler instinct in the dark—
Siberia, Africa, and back—
phosphor runways guiding us to shore,
moonlight half eaten by the waves.

Across the lawn, a lit window floats.
Welts of lupine. You remember
an open window, Arabian music
through wet beeches. We know we're moving
at tremendous speed, that if it could be seen
the stars would be a smear
of velocity. But all is still,
pinioned. In the night garden,
light is a swallowed cry.
Naked in the middle of the city
the stars grow firm in our mouths.

Into Arrival

It will be in a station
with a glass roof
grimy with the soot
of every train and
they will embrace for every mile
of arrival. They will not
let go, not all the long way,
his arm in the curve
of her longing. Walking in a city
neither knows too well,
watching women with satchels
give coins to a priest for the war veterans;
finding the keyhole view of the church
from an old wall across the city, the dome
filling the keyhole precisely,
like an eye. In the home
of winter, under an earth
of blankets, he warms her skin
as she climbs in from the air.

There is a way our bodies
are not our own, and when he finds her
there is room at last
for everyone they love,
the place he finds,
she finds, each word of skin
a decision.

There is earth
that never leaves your hands,

rain that never leaves
your bones. Words so old they are broken
from us, because they can only be
broken. They will not
let go, because some love
is broken from love,
like stones
from stone,
rain from rain,
like the sea
from the sea.

Wild Horses

Minarets of burdock
clang in the copper marsh, the grapes'
frozen skins flood with sweetness.
Winter trees burned to black wicks.

Harnessed, longing cuts
with every turn. Time has one direction,
to divide. Invisible, it casts shadow
canyons, tools furrows into leather fields,
carves oxbow rivers of birds
into cold November skies.

Then, the first stars' faint static,
the sacred transmissions, the hair's
breadth of the intimate
infinite. Iron-oxide sun stains travertine sky,
sudden colour like the ochre
horses of Dordogne, stampeding into lamplight.
Liquid grasses overflow like dark ale.
Twilight is a cave, pungent
with wet hides, torches of resin.

Under the pulling moon, the strap of river
digs into the flesh of field.

There Is No City That Does Not Dream

There is no city that does not dream
from its foundations. The lost lake
crumbling in the hands of brickmakers,
the floor of the ravine where light lies broken
with the memory of rivers. All the winters
stored in that geologic
garden. Dinosaurs sleep in the subway
at Bloor and Shaw, a bed of bones
under the rumbling track. The storm
that lit the city with the voltage
of spring, when we were eighteen
on the clean earth. The ferry ride in the rain,
wind wet with wedding music and everything that
sings in the carbon of stone and bone
like a page of love, wind-lost from a hand, unread.

Last Night's Moon

*"When will we next walk together
under last night's moon?"*
—TU FU

March aspens, mist
forest. Green rain pins down
the sea, early evening
cyanotype. Silver saltlines, weedy
toques of low tide, pillow lava's
black spill indelible
in the sand. Unbroken
broken sea.

   •

Rain sharpens marsh-hair
birth-green of the spring firs.
In the bog where the dead never disappear,
where river birch drown, the surface
strewn with reflection. This is the acid-soaked
moss that eats bones, keeps flesh;
the fermented ground where time stops and
doesn't; dissolves the skull, preserves
the brain, wrinkled pearl in black mud.

   •

In the autumn that made love
necessary, we stood in rubber boots
on the sphagnum raft and learned
love is soil—stronger than peat or sea—
melting what it holds.

The past
is not our own. Mole's ribbon of earth,

termite house,
soaked sponge. It rises,
keloids of rain on wood; spreads,
milkweed galaxy, broken pod
scattering the debris of attention.
Where you are
while your body is here, remembering
in the cold spring afternoon.

The past
is a long bone.

        •

Time is like the painter's lie, no line
around apple or along thigh, though the apple
aches to its sweet edge, strains
to its skin, the seam
of density. Invisible line
closest to touch. Line of wet grass
on my arm, your tongue's
wet line across my back.

All the history in the bone-embedded hills
of your body. Everything your mouth
remembers. Your hands manipulate
in the darkness, silver bromide
of desire darkening skin with light.

        •

Disoriented at great depths,
confused by the noise of shipping routes,

whales hover, small eyes squinting as they consult
the magnetic map of the ocean floor. They strain,
a thousand miles through cold channels;
clicking thrums of distant loneliness
bounce off seamounts and abyssal plains. They look up
from perpetual dusk to rods of sunlight,
a solar forest at the surface.

Transfixed in the dark summer
kitchen: feet bare on humid
linoleum, cilia listening. Feral
as the infrared aura of the snake's prey, the bees'
pointillism, the infrasonic
hum of the desert heard by birds.

The nighthawk spans the ceiling;
swoops. Hot kitchen air
vibrates. I look up
to the pattern of stars under its wings.

.

If love wants you; if you've been melted
down to stars, you will love
with lungs and gills, with warm blood
and cold. With feathers and scales.
Under the hot gloom of the forest canopy
you'll want to breathe with the spiral
calls of birds, while your lashing tail
still gropes for the waves. You'll try
to haul your weight from simple sea
to gravity of land. Caught by the tide,

in the snail-slip of your own path, for moments
suffocating in both water and air.
If love wants you, suddenly your past is
obsolete science. Old maps,
disproved theories, a diorama.

The moment our bodies are set to spring open.
The immanence that reassembles matter
passes through us then disperses
into time and place:
the spasm of fur stroked upright; shocked electrons.
The mother who hears her child crying upstairs
and suddenly feels her dress
wet with milk.
Among black branches, oyster-coloured fog
tongues every corner of loneliness we never knew
before we were loved there,
the places left fallow when we're born,
waiting for experience to find its way
into us. The night crossing, on deck
in the dark car. On the beach where
night reshaped your face.
In the lava fields, carbon turned to carpet,
moss like velvet spread over splintered forms.

The instant spray freezes
in air above the falls, a gasp of ice.
We rise, hearing our names
called home through salmon-blue dusk, the royal moon

an escutcheon on the shield of sky.
The current that passes through us, radio waves,
electric lick. The billions of photons that pass
through film emulsion every second, the single
submicroscopic crystal struck
that becomes the photograph.
We look and suddenly the world
looks back.
A jagged tube of ions pins us to the sky.

.

But if, like starlings, we continue to navigate
by the rear-view mirror
of the moon; if we continue to reach
both for salt and for the sweet white
nibs of grass growing closest to earth;
if, in the autumn bog red with sedge we're also
driving through the canyon at night,
all around us the hidden glow of limestone
erased by darkness; if still we wish
we'd waited for morning,
we will know ourselves
nowhere.
Not in the mirrors of waves
or in the corrading stream,
not in the wavering
glass of an apartment building,
not in the looming light of night lobbies
or on the rainy deck. Not in the autumn kitchen

or in the motel where we watched meteors
from our bed while your slow film, the shutter open,
turned stars to rain.

We will become
indigestible. Afraid
of choking on fur
and armour, animals
will refuse the divided longings
in our foreign blue flesh.

•

In your hands, all you've lost,
all you've touched.
In the angle of your head,
every vow and
broken vow. In your skin,
every time you were disregarded,
every time you were received.
Sundered, drowsed. A seeded field,
mossy cleft, tidal pool, milky stem.
The branch that's released when the bird lifts
or lands. In a summer kitchen.
On a white winter morning, sunlight across the bed.

•

Try to keep everything and keep
standing. In the tall grass,
ten thousand shadows. What's past,
all you've been,
will continue its half-life,

a carbon burn searing its way to heaven
through the twisted core of a pine.
At night, memory will roam your skin.
Your dreams will reveal the squirming world
under the lifted stone.
While you sleep, the sea
floods your house, you wake
to silt, long brown weeds
tangled in the sheets. You wake
in the bog, caked with the froth of peat,
stunted as shore pine,
growing a metre a century.

The bog bruised with colour,
muskeg, hardpan, muck.
Matted green sphagnum
thick as buffalo fur.
Sinking into, buoyed
by spongy ground;
walking on water.

In time, night after night,
we'll begin to dream of a langsam sea,
waves in slow motion, thickening to sand.
Drenched with satiety we'll be slow
to rise, a metre a century.

Our brown bed is peat,
born of water, flooded,
burning with the smell of earth.

The Passionate World

is round. For days we sail, for months,
and still the way is new; strange stars.
Drawn to you, taut over time,
ropes connect this floating floor
to the wind, fraying into sound.

To arrive is to sleep
where we stop moving.
Past the shoal of clothes
to that shore, heaped with debris
of words. A hem of salt,
white lace, on sea-heavy legs.

Love longs for land. All night
we dream the jungle's sleepy electricity;
gnashing chords of insects swim in our ears
and we go under, into green. All night
love draws its heavy drape of scent against the sea
and we wake with the allure of earth in our lungs,
hungry for bread and oranges.
Salamanders dart from your step's shadow, disappear
among wild coffee, fleshy cacti, thorny succulents and
flowers like bowls to save the rain.
We are sailors who wake when the moon intrudes
the smoky tavern of dreams, wake to find a name on an arm
or our bodies bruised by sun or the pressure of a hand,
wake with the map of night on our skin,
traced like moss-stained stone.

Lost, past the last familiar outpost,
flat on deck, milky light cool on our damp hair,
we look up past the ship's angles to stars austere
as a woodcut, and pray we never reach
the lights of that invisible city, where,

landlocked, they have given up on our return.
But some nights, woken by wind,
looking up at different stars,
they are reminded of us, the faint taste of
salt on their lips.

II

The Second Search

"Yesterday at the cemetery, I did not succeed in understanding the words 'Pierre Curie' engraved on the stone."
—MARIE CURIE, 1906

The truth likes to hide
out in the open. Even then,
alone on the bridge, in the solitude
of desire, our moon flooded
the gorges of Truyère. Even then
the satin muscle of a melody
twisted over water, waiting
to be heard: over the Wisła, the Bièvre,
the Seine. Rain tugged with invisible hands
on cedar beards, dug into riverbanks,
squeezed the smell of earth in its fists—
as if it knew someday I'd reach
into powdery brown ore
flecked with needles of Bohemian pines,
stand forty-five months under umbrellas or wet
under sun, stirring the blue spirit
from the bitter breath of pitchblende.
So much to burn through, years, to reach
that colour. As if Polish rain already knew
our flooded garden in Paris: I waited
while you were carried
home from Rue Dauphine, half your skull
hardened into pavement; moonlight's blade
against the throats of flowers, pink flesh
soaked, purple mouths open,
shouts turned to dust on their tongues.
Sepia damp like the forests of Minière and Port Royale
you'd described, guiding me to sleep: even then

instructing me not to fear
the ground, to give thanks
to the worm-churned paths
of failure that brought us together,
to refuse the shroud, cover you instead
with hawthorne, iris, the black cloth
of earth you loved.

Before we married
I stood above the river
pulling at my hands
as if I'd already lost something so beautiful
my skin was stained. How similar
the leap of faith and the leap
of fear. While a bird
signed its name on the sky. Even then
I felt you through my clothes, like the radium kiss
through Becquerel's vest pocket, the kiss he never forgot,
burning into his belly.

I pulled apart your coat
looking for you. I kissed your cloth shadow and kept
your blood under my nails. I screamed at Irène
for closing a book you'd left open on a table.

The longer we lived together, the more
I loved you. Day after day
I poured something purer
into basins and jars. I watched you
bent over your table like a jeweller,

setting things that can't be seen. The joy
of concentration, the elements
love precipitates to. By then our hands
never stopped moving, our skin
was wool, long gloves eating us
to the bone. We opened the door to
the aurora borealis, to icebergs, to distant
mountains lining the shelves.
The blue residue that clings like scent,
fogs everything with its breath.
At night, at work, we sat as if
under stars. The glowing distillation
of time.

You laughed when I marked cookbooks
with the same care as notes in the lab
but for me it was the same: the same
details of love—dissolving, filtering, collecting
until truth is so small it fits
on the tongue. My body sore from standing
in the yard, stirring. Or from stretching
under you.
Night sounds on the lawn
at Sceaux, lamps on the porch,
wooden legs scraping flagstones
as your father followed the moon with his chair.
Listening to a song on dark drifts over the river
knowing there was no difference, your hand
asleep on my side, whether you were thinking
of essential salts or atomic numbers or the secret

effects of moonlight: it was the same love,
radiant with memory, simple as skin.

Everything we touch
burns away, whether we give ourselves
or not, the same April day spreads to thinness,
the same winter afternoon
thickens to dark. I was thirty-eight years old.
Every time a door opened
I expected you. For months I hid your clothes
stiff with blood.
Only the street understood. I walked
and shut my eyes, gave myself up to the God
of trams, horses, cabs.

You are the glass that silences
wet leaves, the silence of the winter river.
I no longer see the world
with your eyes, but see you
in the world: invisibility bending the branch;
the moon wobbling, just halved;
skin vanishing under the rays.
When Albert in the middle of a proof
suddenly slung off his rucksack
to stare down the chasms of Engandine,
grabbing my arm, wild: "I need to know
what happens to passengers
when the elevator falls into emptiness"—
and I held our girls, afraid

they'd laugh themselves over the edge—
it was you I'd been thinking of,
as we crossed the Majola Pass.

I take our daughters
to the rivers you loved.
We walk along the Bièvre
where you spent whole nights
fishing ideas out of the water.
I think of silver skin,
invisible in the current, yet
separating cold bright blood
from the colourless river. Invisible
as oxygen sealing water and ice,
so the line between river and sky
won't break, hydrogen aligning itself
in one direction, under skaters' blades.
Moving faster with each slow stride.
Nothing warms like motion,
speed in our thighs.

I can only find you
by looking deeper, that's how love
leads us into the world.

My hands burn
all the time.

Ice House

"I regret nothing but his suffering."
—KATHLEEN SCOTT

Wherever we cry,
it's far from home.

    •

At Sandwich, our son pointed
persistently to sea.
I followed his infant gaze,
expecting a bird or a boat
but there was nothing.
How unnerving,
as if he could see you
on the horizon,
knew where you were
exactly:
at the edge of the world.

    •

You unloaded the ship at Lyttelton
and repacked her:

"thirty-five dogs
five tons of dog food
fifteen ponies
thirty-two tons of pony fodder
three motor-sledges
four hundred and sixty tons of coal
collapsible huts

an acetylene plant
thirty-five thousand cigars
one guinea pig
one fantail pigeon
three rabbits
one cat with its own hammock, blanket and pillow
one hundred and sixty-two carcasses of mutton and
an ice house"

•

Men returned from war
without faces, with noses lost
discretely as antique statues,
accurately as if eaten
by frostbite.
In clay I shaped their
flesh, sometimes
retrieving a likeness
from photographs.
Then the surgeons copied
nose, ears, jaw
with molten wax and metal plates
and horsehair stitches;
with borrowed cartilage,
from the soldiers' own ribs,
leftovers stored under the skin
of the abdomen. I held the men down
until the morphia

slid into them.
I was only sick
afterwards.

Working the clay, I remembered
mornings in Rodin's studio,
his drawerfuls of tiny hands and feet,
like a mechanic's tool box.
I imagined my mother in her blindness
before she died, touching my face,
as if still she could
build me with her body.

At night, in the studio
I took your face in my hands and your fine
arms and long legs, your small waist,
and loved you into stone.

The men returned from France
to Ellerman's Hospital.
Their courage
was beautiful.
I understood the work at once:
To use scar tissue to advantage.
To construct through art,
one's face to the world.
Sculpt what's missing.

·

You reached furthest south,
then you went further.

In neither of those forsaken places
did you forsake us.

·

At Lyttelton the hills unrolled,
a Japanese scroll painting;
we opened the landscape with our bare feet.

So much learned by observation.
We took in brainfuls of New Zealand air
on the blue climb over the falls.

Our last night together we slept
not in the big house but
in the Kinseys' garden.
Belonging only
to each other.
Guests of the earth.

·

Mid-sea, a month out of range
of the wireless;
on my way to you. Floating
between landfalls,

between one hemisphere and another.
Between the words
"wife" and "widow."

·

Newspapers, politicians
scavenged your journals.

But your words
never lost their way.

·

We mourn in a place no one knows;
it's right that our grief be unseen.

I love you as if you'll return
after years of absence.
As if we'd invented
moonlight.

·

Still I dream
of your arrival.

The Hooded Hawk

for A.W.

*". . . I had come into my own; painful to the extreme limit
of endurance as that place and state might be."*
—KATHLEEN RAINE

History chokes on the little bones
of meaning, the little bones
of love. Early winter, late
afternoon, the room went dark.
We sat a long time
before noticing. You were recounting
a trip to Rome, not the conference
but a woman who remembered those who hid
or fled. You stood to turn on a lamp, instead
sat down again. Your voice
more distinct in darkness.

You knew it like a secret:
the chalk body outlined
under the skin, "the line," you wrote,
between "what's permissible" and "what's
possible." History: the silver spoon
in your kitchen drawer,
swastika on its handle. The "tulips and daffodils"
escaping children were told to run to, who
remember instead "bloodhounds and rats."
Your mother's dolls—all the refugee parts
we're made of. History is the love that enters us
through death; its discipline
is grief. You never forgot the floating ghettos:
landlocked in north Winnipeg, listening with your father

to the radio, while the boat was refused
at every port. Eleven years old,
you were with them, those who had no place,
while the streetcars squealed to a turn
on North Main, and in the front room
the sewing machines and wooden steaming blocks
thudded all night; with them
listening to your mother tell of her
escape across the river—
"we must bring our children to a shore";
and again in '55, alone on deck,
anxious to begin as a writer;
with them when we spoke of
exiled Walter Benjamin, who devoured books
"the way a flame 'reads' wood,"
or when later you wrote of your childhood:
"I belonged where I read."

    •

The dolls your mother made
were stories. "He's the French type . . .
dresses just so . . . he likes to chase after women . . ."
She holds up an Englishman and in her other hand
his pregnant wife: "Now he's more mature
for his responsibilities." When the stories were sad
she dressed them in finery
so we wouldn't turn away. After a pogrom, when she was young,
your mother rooted out buttons and bits of glass,
"scraps of this and that" and never stopped: wooden spools,
used light bulbs, leftover leather, bottle tops,

lids of jars, labels, beads,
bone. Her one requirement: that the object
had lost its purpose. So what was torn
transformed to something whole:
a hat, a foot, a hand.
Your mother sewed all night
and fell asleep on the cutting table.

All your writing life, you worked at night.

•

One Thanksgiving it took two
to carry the platter—your idea,
a cauliflower steamed whole,
cerebral and surreal, regal
as the head of a saint. Elevated
to a centrepiece. I understood the symbol:
they harvested cauliflowers
from the fields near Terezin . . .
At the table, your favourite ghost sat with us,
the poet, Heine, who knew home
is in the mouth: not just language but
carp in raisin sauce, lamb
with horseradish and garlic—
even in Paris, surrounded by *cuisine.*

•

In your unlit apartment.
After another stage of illness.
All the years were with us.

Of your mother's death
you wrote, "My loss is endless . . . its only closure
will be my own." This winter afternoon, two years after
your death, sorrow magnifies
through the generations, each human's part
heaped upon the next, in this way our griefs
are joined. For all the talk,
for all the speaking up and
out, the core sample
is silence. We made a pact
of dusk. In your kitchen so many afternoons,
in your last apartment, in this apartment.
This November afternoon.

•

Almost forty, childless,
so much of your life
given to ghosts. You lived with your story
longer than they were stranded
on that boat, on the verge of war.
Longer than the war.
Years later, you pushed the manuscript across the table
without comment. Your daughter almost as old
as the abandoned pages.

In a dream
the hooded hawk is sometimes
love, sometimes
death; everything stops at the moment
of unmasking.

Colette said, when one we love dies
there's no reason to stop
writing them letters.

Since you died,
love has opened every place
that won't open.

In a dream you said,
I am being reborn in
the womb of the earth.

You were with them,
those without place.

In your last apartment,
early winter
late afternoon.

Your face had the tenderness
of a hand.

III

Fontanelles

> *"How much must be forgotten, out of love,*
> *how much must be forgiven, even love."*
> —W. H. AUDEN, "Canzone"

Chalk and beeches. The winter sea
looks for itself in the new dark,
turning the smallest colour.

We brought our daughter here
before she was mortal. Before I knew
a person can be a prayer. Before
I had ever bathed a child, before
I felt another's death
could be my own.

We've gone on, each year
a little deeper, to the place
where land is geology, where objects are defined
by the space in them.
Where proteins assemble themselves
into souls. We've come in winter,
in the rain. To islands, to the abbey, always
cold, always looking,
to remember. Photographing the ruins
near Roan Fell. At North Beach and
Melmerby Fell. All the places where the earth
crumbles into edges.
The landscapes we saw
from love. From love,
to a marram field roaring under two thousand
Atlantic miles of moonlight, scent scoured
in the salt, as if an invisible woman
embraced us in the dark; the clover's

trace in cow's breath, in sweet milk,
woven by wind into the tall grass,
roots binding the sand. Arable islands
of porous lava, and islands so rigid the rain
bruises into peat, parietal
thumbprints in the gneiss
like the soft lakes
in an infant's skull.

Islands that are outer. Not barren
but precise. Not a wildflower
wasted.

The narrow channel, a gap of two thousand
million years. The inner basalt islands,
a green fifty million years old, where peacocks
fertilized lush gardens, darted
from massive hedges of rhododendron
while sugars and phosphates, thymine and
cytosine, guanine and adenine
aligned and divided with their three degrees of freedom;
in the winter, in the rain.

There is no song the sea
will not put in its mouth.

.

November mountains
the colour of marmalade,
mineral shadows. A thread of road clings
to the coast. Store, hotel, distillery.

The mysterious ways of the peat
can capsize a lorry like a toy;
the tides swallow a boat in seconds.
A glacial sea has nibbled caves and left behind
raised beaches, stranded high above the waves.
From Ardlussa, where the road ends,
seven miles through dense oak forest
to dying Orwell's farm,
the silent eyes of five thousand red deer
surrounding him in the night.

From Ardlussa, where the road ends.

·

Together we've looked to limestone and to apoptosis,
to discarded theories and the Abbés Glory and
Breuil, who followed children into the painted caves
of Altamira and Lascaux. To Jacques Loeb and
Jacques Monod, whose faith was biology,
who knew that awe is like an apple,
sweetest where the light collects,
under the skin. To everything
science breaks open to learn
what's inside, Irène Curie looking for truth
in a block of paraffin. To facts as unprovable
as one's own death. To icebergs
old as stone. To the granite sphinx
and the two-hundred-and-fifty-kilo priest
of Isis,
winched from the dusk
of Alexandria Harbour, from a sea bath

of sixteen hundred years.
And to how long
the handprint has marked the cave,
and to the nine months, and the time
twice that, for the fontanelles to close.

I've watched a woman swim
at North Beach, her pink belly
an eclipse rising from the waves; later,
the story she told, so close to me—
smell of coffee, rattle of ice, soft click
of billiards, through her Europe and her forests—
eager to speak before love made her
forget
where to begin. Long before
the first twenty cells, before
the corpus luteum, before
the microscopic heart,
long before hands and eyes.

I returned to North Beach and to
her words, the lake
winter-empty, tide trailing a branch
along the sand, while neural folds
fused. Before the brain, before gills
became bones or ears; "the ancient
genetic information shared with the fishes."

The distance a child travels,
tens of thousands of years,
one cell at a time. Cells that know

how to heal a wound from seam to seam,
from the depth. Cells that know
to assemble or re-
assemble themselves.
To regenerate blood and skin,
like a starfish that loses its arms
and grows them back again.

The body is a memory palace;
like Simonides' "inner writing,"
where each detail of each room corresponds
to one of the ninety-seven hundred lines
of Virgil's *Aeneid*,
or like tribes who use the whole Sahara
to remember a story.

Entropic catalogue.

The primitive streak, the blood islands.
Blessed protein.

·

We came to photograph night. At the cliff,
to blacken film with the last atoms
of day. Later we'll look with faces
almost to the paper to see the waves,
creases of shadow darker than the dark
unlocking. Recall our
invisibility,
but for our white
breath.

A task, this waiting
for the dark, the slow disintegration
of sunlight, impossible to record
the moment one overtakes the other,
as it is to name the moment embryo
becomes foetus; the only time of day
quantum theory seems reasonable. When sight
is feeling. I think of Heisenberg's twilight
walks in Faelled Park, determined
to rid the universe of waves,
holding his head, minding terribly
his p's and q's. Or walking Copenhagen's
Langelinie, watching a freighter "fabulous
and unreal in the bright blue dusk . . .
biological laws exerting their powers
not merely on protein molecules but
on steel and electric currents . . ."
Or at four a.m. on the roof reading
Plato's *Timaeus*, neither
day nor night, the moment he knew
"that the smallest particles of matter
must reduce to a mathematical form."

Like sacred sites built from secular
stones—the priory filched from Hadrian's Wall,
or the Cistercian monastery built around pagan
altars to Jupiter and Silvanus—
spirit snags in the quantum mechanism.
Daughter cells, organelles, morula.
The shape of the belly

becomes the shape of the head.
From Ardlussa to North Beach.
From stones to atoms.
From atoms to stones.

The chemistry of looking;
to look until the river
swallows us, until the redness
of the stone fills our veins.
To look until we're
seen. But this is only longing.
We leave our heat shadows
in moss shocked with frost.
Even your camera
sees more; the detail you crave.
We strain to see even
what the camera sees,
what the eye can't; and this is as good
as a philosophy. An embrace
of failure, as if
just once, impossibly,
we'll catch the visible reflection
of what's invisible.
Our white breath in the dark.

How to photograph this,
the dark when one has said
too much. The dark
of sudden feeling. Love's
darkness.

The sea, folded paper;
rain filling each crease.
A twist of bright salt,
a twist of foam.
Phosphene.

Dark with hope.

.

A winter Sunday.
On the surface,
pilgrims to limestone, the cavers lay,
the earth's breath in their hair,
the breath of profound darkness,
ten metres and thirty thousand
years. Headfirst,
they dove into the draught.

They shouted into a chamber
too deep for lamps to grasp,
a sweating mineral space
white as exposed film in the darkness.
They unfurled a black plastic path
across the glinting calcite floor;
so their progress wouldn't disturb
the scattered bones and teeth and
tracks of ancient animals.

Aurochs and mammoths in charcoal and ochre.
In the gallery of horses

they shouted without words,
their joy
unpronounceable.

Near their feet,
under the gaze of pensive horses,
the imprint of two hands.

They ascended into the clean
chill of the gorge, dusk,
fine cold starlight
crystallizing their breath.
Dazed, they could only descend again.
And again, into the smell of wet clay;
the third time through the passage,
almost midnight, at last
bringing one who wouldn't believe
without seeing it herself—
a caver's daughter.

"We had lost all track of time."

·

You carry your camera
under the earth.

Rain wounds the snow. Gashes of mud
blacken a path. We light the lamps
and dive. Your sixty trillion cells
and mine. In the caves of Aldène and

Fontanet, paleolithic children played
while their parents painted. Small knee
prints and footprints in the clay.
Thousands of years later, the children return:
Maria who found the bison
on Altamira's stone sky;
Marcel who followed his dog, Robot,
into the mouth of Lascaux.

After eight weeks, the hands.
A mouth without lips.

After twenty-five weeks, filaments
follow a trail of chemical
scent through the cortex,
wiring up ears and eyes.
After thirty weeks, quantum whispering:
thought.

·

Almost in deference
to geologic time,
it takes generations
to become an islander.
Only ghosts earn a place.

The wind scrubs the air so clear
even the most crowded heart
remembers all it loves.

·

We bathe our daughter,
a prayer for every part,
as if we were washing her
with song.
Fingers frail as blades of grass.
Her thousands of eggs,
already inside her.

•

To love as if we'd choose
even the grief.

•

All love is time travel.

Scoured shore, painted caves,
limestone gorges.
Plums and cold water in the desert.

The winter river. This far.

A Note on the Text

Sublimation

Writer Alfred Döblin, perhaps best known for his novel *Berlin Alexander-platz*, escaped Germany during the Second World War; he was one of the few exiled writers who made the difficult decision to return after the war. The poem's "shadow bride" was photographer Yolla Niclas.

A Lesson from the Earth

Johannes Kepler (1571–1630) pursued mathematical harmonies in a Europe torn by the counter-reformation and the Thirty Years War. His Three Laws freed thought by marrying astronomy and physics for the first time, paving the way directly for Newton's theory of gravity. By proving that planets follow elliptical, not circular, orbits, he dismantled a false and cumbersome view of the solar system, which had been tied to theology. He met and worked with Danish astronomer Tycho Brahe in 1600, a year before Tycho's death. Brahe's remarkably accurate observational data was published later in the Rudolphine Tables, named for Emperor Rudolph II, the patron of both Brahe and Kepler.

Modersohn–Becker

German painter Paula Becker (1876–1907) regarded both commitments—family duty and her art—with equal seriousness; her short life was marked by a wrenching struggle between the two. She left the artists' colony of Worp-swede, where she'd been living with her husband, the painter Otto Moder-sohn, for Paris. She returned to the marriage and later that year, at age thirty-one, she died suddenly, shortly after giving birth to their only child.

Blue Vigour

Before she became the highly acclaimed short-story writer, using the pen name Isak Dinesen, Karen Blixen emigrated from Denmark to Kenya, where she ran a farm from 1913 to 1931. Her love and respect for the land and its people are documented in her paintings and memoirs.

Stone

Lunia Czechowska, a Russian émigré, met the Italian painter Amedeo Modigliani in Paris in 1917, three years before his death. At the time, Modigliani was living with the painter Jeanne Hébuterne.

What the Light Teaches

Marina Tsvetaeva, Osip Mandelstam, and Anna Akhmatova—three of Russia's best-known modern poets—suffered profoundly during the Stalinist regime. In order that their words not be lost to censorship, enforced exile, and imprisonment, friends and family often memorized complete poems. In Mandelstam's case, the poems were preserved in his wife Nadezhda's memory and survived even while the poet himself perished in a labour camp.

The Second Search

The Polish physicist Marie Sklodowska Curie (1867–1934) and her husband, the French physicist Pierre Curie, shared an intense and productive parnership, both in their marriage and in their professional lives. In 1903, they earned a Nobel Prize for Physics for their discovery of radium, together with the French scientist Henri Becquerel. When Pierre Curie died suddenly, in a traffic accident in Paris, Marie Curie began a private journal, "the grey notebooks," where she wrote out her grief.

Ice House

Kathleen Scott was a sculptor, and the wife of the Antarctic explorer Robert Falcon Scott. They had been married two years, with an eleven-month-old son, when Scott went south to the Pole. Upon parting in New Zealand, they made a pact to keep a daily journal for each other. Scott perished on the return journey from the Pole, and when his body and the bodies of his companions were found in the spring, his diary was brought back to England. On the inside cover, Scott had written "Send this diary to my wife." Then Scott drew a line through the word "wife" and wrote instead, "widow."

Acknowledgments

Thanks to the editors of the magazines and anthologies where versions of some of these poems first appeared. From *The Weight of Oranges: Writ, Waves, Poetry Toronto,* and *Poetry Canada Review;* from *Miner's Pond: Saturday Night, The Malahat Review,* and *What* magazine; from *Skin Divers: Border Crossings, Event, Arc, Toronto Life, Windhorse Reader, Slow Dancer, Fish Drum, We Who Can Fly,* and *Border Lines: Contemporary Poems in English.* "There Is No City That Does Not Dream" appeared as part of the Toronto Transit Commission's *Poetry on the Way* program.

The quotation in "Miner's Pond" on page 61 is from John Noble Wilford's *The Riddle of the Dinosaur,* on page 64 from John McLoughlin's *Synapsida: A New Look into the Origin of Mammals,* and on pages 65–6 from Timothy Ferris's *Coming of Age in the Milky Way.* The quotations in "The Hooded Hawk" on pages 173–6 are from Adele Wiseman's *Old Woman at Play.* The quotation in "Fontanelles" on page 184 is from Boyce Rensberger's *Life Itself,* and on page 189 from *Dawn of Art* by Jean-Marie Chauvet, Eliette Deschamps, and Christian Hillaire.

My thanks to the authors of books that were especially helpful in the research of various poems; for "The Second Search," *Marie Curie,* by Eve Curie; and for "Ice House," *A Great Task of Happiness,* by Louisa Young, from which the list of the *Terra Nova*'s supplies were itemized. "Pillar of Fire" is based on the log entries of Captain Watson, of the H.M.S. *Charles Bal.*

"What the Light Teaches" is for Janis Freedman. "Fresh Mint" is for Vivian Palin.

Many thanks to Sonny Mehta.
Thanks to Ellen Seligman. And to Heather Sangster.
Thanks to Marilyn Biderman.
Thanks to David Laurence.
Thanks to T. F. & P. And to John.

A NOTE ON THE TYPE

This book was set in Minion, a typeface produced by the Adobe Corporation specifically for the Macintosh personal computer and released in 1990. Designed by Robert Slimbach, Minion combines the classic characteristics of old-style faces with the full complement of weights required for modern typesetting.

Composed by NK Graphics,
Keene, New Hampshire
Printed and bound by Quebecor Printing,
Fairfield, Pennsylvania
Designed by Virginia Tan